# Routledge
Taylor & Francis Group

LONDON AND NEW YORK

# Primary EAL Provision

Getting it right ✓

# IN A WEEK

**Kirsty Anderson**
Series editor: **Susan Wallace**

First published in 2018 by Critical Publishing Ltd.

Published 2025 by Routledge
4 Park Square, Milton Park, Abingdon, Oxon OX14 4RN
605 Third Avenue, New York, NY 10017

*Routledge is an imprint of the Taylor & Francis Group,
an informa business*

British Library Cataloguing in Publication Data
A CIP record for this book is available from the British Library

ISBN: 9781912096893 (pbk)
ISBN: 9781041056560 (ebk)

The right of Kirsty Anderson to be identified as the Author of this
work have been asserted by her in accordance with the Copyright,
Design and Patents Act 1988.

Cartoons © 2018 Michael Wallace
Cover and text design by Out of House Limited

DOI: 10.4324/9781041056560

# CONTENTS

## Meet the author

Kirsty Anderson

*I am a Teaching Fellow in the School of Education at Durham University, teaching English and Art for Education on the undergraduate programme. I am also the departmental co-ordinator for Erasmus and international opportunities. I worked in Newcastle schools for 14 years as class teacher, literacy consultant and deputy head. I have extensive experience of working with children who have English as an additional language through working in diverse, multicultural schools. I am currently attempting to learn Czech while also undertaking a PhD exploring the demands of teaching profession.*

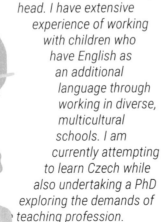

## Meet the series editor

Susan Wallace

*I am Emeritus Professor of Education at Nottingham Trent University where part of my role has been to support trainee teachers on initial and in-service teacher training courses. My own experience of classroom teaching has been mainly with 14 to 19 year olds; I have also worked in a local authority advisory role for this age group. My particular interest is in the motivation and behaviour management of reluctant and disengaged learners, and I've written a number of books and research papers on this topic. My work allows me the privilege of meeting, observing and listening to teachers from all sectors of education. It is to them that I owe many of the tips and ideas contained in these pages.*

# Introduction

An internationally focused and culturally aware classroom might be easy to picture: globes and maps on display highlighting the home countries of some learners; international links made by the institution; dual language notices and labels; a teacher regularly greeting learners in different languages reflecting the mother tongue of the varied learners. Without doubt this classroom would feel welcoming and begin to establish a global citizenship ethos and a multicultural environment. What is next though? If learners feel welcome and safe in this setting, as indeed the Teachers' Standards indicate they should, how do you take this forward to foster language acquisition and academic success in English as an additional language (EAL) learners? While a new starter might be encouraged and comfortable in such a classroom, this only scratches the surface of successful work with EAL learners. An effective teacher will aim to move beyond the surface and offer them opportunities to develop a depth of understanding equal to their native English-speaking peers.

Central to your success when teaching EAL learners is remembering that EAL is not a subject. It might seem silly to highlight this but it is easy to confuse EAL with EFL – English as a foreign language, lessons for which you would be very likely to find in major cities around the world. Though there may be many similarities in the English language lessons, EFL lessons are designed around learning English. EAL learners on the other hand are most likely to be learning English *and* other curriculum subjects – effectively learning new concepts in a new language. You therefore need to carefully consider the language needs of the subject you are teaching, remembering that the EAL learners will be taught this subject in a language different from their mother tongue. Don't forget that your EAL learners are keeping up with the moving target of their native English peers. Quite a challenging task for these learners really!

Many teachers will find themselves working with EAL learners at some point. For some this may include working within multicultural communities – meaning the number of such learners in the class may be high – while others may work with only a handful of EAL learners in their careers. Whichever group you fall into, your priority will be the same: ensuring that all learners make progress in using and understanding specific subject knowledge and developing English language skills. This book aims to focus on this through offering a toolkit of strategies and suggestions useful in different scenarios for a range of different EAL learners. The book is written to be explored and understood in just one week. It concisely addresses the challenges of EAL learners in a practical rather than theoretical way while at the same time showing how the suggested strategies are underpinned by sound theory. Each *Spot of theory* is designed to point you towards key thinking in this field, which will both further your understanding and provide useful sources to inform assessed work if you are working towards, for example, an initial or additional teaching qualification.

The book is aimed at all teachers who would like to improve their teaching strategies for working with EAL learners either because they are already engaged with this group of learners or because they realise that they will, at some point, find these skills useful. In a working paper, NALDIC (1999) identified five areas of a *Distinctive EAL Pedagogy*. The five areas suggested are:

1. activating prior knowledge;
2. provision of a rich context;
3. encouraging comprehensible input;

4. making grammatical form and function explicit;

5. developing learner independence.

You might recognise the value of these five areas as relevant to the planning for any learner. They are the areas which underpin many of the ideas and suggestions offered in the pages which follow.

Whether you are a trainee or an experienced teacher, there are many ideas here to help you and your EAL learners succeed. This book uses the term 'learner' rather than 'pupil' or 'student'. The term 'learner' is a useful reminder for you about the goal of your classroom.

It is important to remember that EAL learners are not a single, homogenous group. Not only are there, of course, a multitude of different languages – according to NALDIC (2016) up to 360 languages are spoken in the UK – but there are also a number of different levels or standards which the EAL learners may demonstrate in the classroom. The standards range from new-to-English learners with little or no English vocabulary to advanced bilinguals who are fluent speakers and writers in both English and their mother tongue. The strategies presented in this book can be utilised across this wide-ranging group. Some may be more suitable for new starters, but you will find that even the most advanced EAL learner might benefit from some of the more distinctive EAL-specific pedagogy presented here.

The key aim of this book is to introduce you to strategies which will help you to ensure that the EAL learners in your classroom are learning alongside their peers rather than separately. On occasion it can be helpful to introduce a strategy to a small group or one-to-one. However, the goal is to provide suggestions which can facilitate teaching and learning for all. The book includes tried and tested strategies and information which can help your understanding of EAL learners and their learning needs. This is important as you develop your teaching skills as it can ensure that you are able to manage your classroom effectively as a learning space without feeling anxious that any learners are left behind.

The seven chapters of the book develop your skill set and understanding in a logical sequence. **Day 1** includes a range of strategies for getting started with EAL learners. These are specifically designed for busy teachers to enable all class members to continue to learn and importantly to get EAL learners to start talking; this will be useful as the learners demonstrate the skills which are the focus of **Day 2**: reading and writing. This chapter helps you understand which aspects of English can be particularly difficult for EAL learners. Language and literacy skills across the curriculum are the aim of **Day 3**, giving you further strategies to support learner understanding. **Day 4** takes the previous chapters further by considering planning and differentiation specifically for EAL learners to promote the central aim of engagement. On **Day 5** you will see a range of useful ways to engage families as well as suggestions for working collaboratively with other adults in your classroom. **Day 6** presents strategies for checking, recording and monitoring progress in effective ways for this group of learners. Finally, **Day 7** outlines some of the challenges faced by EAL learners, and how you might support and celebrate these to make your classroom a welcoming multicultural space for learning.

For those of you who are very short of time, you'll find near the end of each chapter a single suggested strategy from those included under the heading *If you only try one thing from this chapter, try this*. At the very end of each chapter is a checklist which facilitates a record of what worked well for you and with whom.

This book is planned to be easily accessed, easy to use and easily applicable to your own practice and experience. Some of the scenarios may feel daunting; some may be very familiar while others may simply be interesting! The goal of this book is to support you to teach EAL learners effectively with strategies which can help both you and your learners to succeed.

## Engaging EAL learners from the outset: initial and immediate strategies for support

Day 1 of this book is focused on initial strategies to ensure language learning and high expectations from the outset. You might be nervous about working with learners who are learning English as an additional language (EAL) as you will be teaching these learners in English rather than their mother tongue. You might anticipate a silent period for some learners as they become familiar with the environment. This is certainly possible, but in Day 1 you will find some suggestions to encourage talking and taking part which aim to engage the learners and help you to observe their progress. In relation to developing EAL, continued practice really does make perfect! EAL learners, from those who are new to English to advanced bilingual learners, acquire more proficiency at, and understanding of, English daily. New vocabulary can be shared with home, where it can be practised. Recording devices can be helpful with this. The mother tongue will of course lead conversations at home, but sharing the daily language gains with family and friends can ensure that home involvement is expected, encouraged, valued and indeed essential.

Establishing high expectations as EAL learners move forward in their English language acquisition and understanding will help to ensure that you and your learners recognise that progress is important. Immediate support and encouragement can ensure that the EAL learners are developing language skills without delay; it can help you ensure the learner has meaningful and productive tasks; and, most importantly, it can indicate clearly what the learner already knows.

**Making the right start – a welcome pack:**
1. Navigating the day
2. Survival language
3. Comprehensible cultural contexts

**Time to talk:**
4. Practising vocabulary
5. Thinking and talking time
6. Pick up a sticky note

**Opening up questions:**
7. Listening
8. Learner-led questioning
9. Enabling options

**Peer support:**
10. All about us
11. Language partners
12. Practice partners

## Strategy: Making the right start – a welcome pack

With some careful consideration, the initial experiences of an EAL learner can be made much more comfortable with a welcome pack which includes navigation tools, survival language, other vocabulary, links with the home country and a recording device. A pack which includes information on timetables, uniforms if applicable, lunch arrangements and essential equipment would be useful for any new starter but can be helpfully adapted for EAL learners.

### 1. Navigating the day

A timetable of the school day can be made more readable by including a map; photographs of the entrance to buildings, cloakroom areas and break spaces would ensure this is understood in any language. If a school uniform or any special equipment is needed then you can include pictures of these to further illustrate what is required.

### 2. Survival language

To make certain the EAL learner, and in particular a new-to-English learner, has a smooth transition, the welcome pack can be made even more specific to their needs. You can include lists of key vocabulary, such as the names of equipment and clothing. You can also include important phrases that will aid the learner; for example: *I need help* or *Where is the bathroom?* Making a keyring of this and other survival language with clear pictures will help you communicate immediately with your EAL learners.

### 3. Comprehensible cultural contexts

This context-related thought process is vital when you plan learning opportunities for EAL learners, especially when teaching more abstract concepts. Your EAL learners will be learning English in their second language. When teaching reading, writing, speaking and listening it is useful to have a context onto which the learners can hang their understanding. You can link reading to the learners' interests to provide a context and ask for writing about their own experiences, for example. As the EAL learner becomes more competent and confident, the high context-based learning can be gradually reduced.

*Provide a welcome pack for all new EAL learners.*

Every Wednesday new starters are welcomed into Marie's primary school. She decided to make sure she was always prepared with her ready supply of personalised welcome packs. For the Year 2 learners in her class, Marie includes name labels for the new starters' coats and storage as well as the information provided by the administration team. Keeping high expectations in mind, she includes a picture book as well as a reading book in each welcome pack. To ensure the EAL learner is made to feel especially welcome and then hopefully settles in more quickly, Marie finds out a little about the home country of the new starter. She includes key vocabulary in the mother tongue, and looks for a cultural reference for the country. Marie includes an aspect of popular culture from the home country in order to ensure that the new starter recognises that their new class is interested in increasing an understanding of different countries in order to firmly develop a global perspective.

On one particular Wednesday, Maroš, from the Czech Republic, was starting in her class at age seven. Marie looked at Czech TV children's programmes and discovered *Krtek* – a little mole. Krtek is widely known and very popular in the Czech Republic. She downloaded an image and made a bookmark for Maroš. Maroš and his family were understandably anxious about his start, especially as he did not attend formal schooling in the Czech Republic which starts when children are aged seven. They were thrilled to see the popular culture reference included in his pack. The family talked about Krtek animatedly and through observing their facial expressions and gestures Marie felt confident that Maroš would feel a little less anxiety about the new start. Others in the class also showed interest, making sure Maroš' home country became a talking point – showing that Marie and her learners respect and value each other and the wider world.

### A spot of theory

*In the 1980s Stephen Krashen began to explore how second languages were acquired. His influential work highlighted the value of comprehensible input for EAL learners. If learning has a connection to the experiences of the EAL learner through recognisable pictures or diagrams, for example, then this can help learners to understand the message being communicated.*

## Strategy: Time to talk

Writing is one of the main ways of assessing independent understanding in education but this is closely linked to speech and language. Encouraging EAL learners to engage in opportunities to talk can increase confidence and help to develop English vocabularies that can be applied to developing writing skills, which will be explored on Day 2 of this book. Moreover, through encouraging talk about the learners' developing reading and writing skills you can assess knowledge and understanding more quickly than you might if you are focused on reading and writing skills alone.

### 4. Practising vocabulary

Vocabulary sets can be produced around various themes. New-to-English learners can be taught high frequency words (which can be found in *Letters & Sounds* [2007], available in many staff rooms as well as online) and lists can be taken home for more practice. You can introduce new sets when the learner demonstrates their recognition of the vocabulary through blending sounds and sight reading. Sets of vocabulary can also be linked to topics or themes. Organising vocabulary sets into different word classes, for instance: nouns, verbs, adjectives, prepositions, can be particularly helpful for the EAL learner if it is common for their mother tongue or home language to be taught this way.

### 5. Thinking and talking time

When you ask questions or open a discussion, give ample time for thinking, and facilitate this with useful vocabulary and sentence prompts as well as talking through thoughts. Your EAL learners need to process their

understanding in both English and their mother tongue and then aim to explain their thoughts in English. To ensure all learners have the time to respond to you, you might use an egg-timer as part of your regular practice. You might expect more detailed or complicated responses from a native English speaker or an advanced bilingual learner. New-to-English learners' responses may be less complex but giving time for thinking will help their internal dialogue and gives you time to appreciate the processes involved in dual language learning.

### 6. Pick up a sticky note

When opportunities for talk are offered in your lessons, it is useful to listen to the language utilised by the learners. Using sticky notes you can quickly jot down any English words or phrases which are used by the EAL learners. You might even enlist other learners to make notes of these, and eventually encourage the EAL learner to note the words they have used from their own vocabulary list. If you observe and listen to the new-to-English learner as they work with others you will quickly find out what language they already have, and with more advanced EAL learners you can listen for specific aspects of English which might be proving difficult, such as subject – verb agreement or past tense formation.

✸ Look at the notes made by this teacher in observations of some learners working as a group to classify art works during a Year 4 art lesson. Consider what the teacher can assess about the two EAL learners' language skills.

| Learner | First language | Notes |
|---------|----------------|-------|
| Shelina | Bengali | *Shelina checked the vocabulary list before examining the pictures. She said the words out loud to Ruby to check her pronunciation but then no longer needed the checklist. Shelina used some specific art terms correctly:* line, colour, tone *and* shade. |
| Ruby | English | *Clear and correct use of the appropriate art vocabulary. Helped Shelina to form past tense of* shade. |
| Marianka | Slovakian | *Good eye contact with the others. Marianka answered a question directed at her by Ruby about the colours in the painting. She used the vocabulary list with matching pictures to say:* red, green, blue. |

Shelina is a confident English speaker. She does need some support and would benefit from regular 'pre-teaching' (perhaps through homework) of key vocabulary.

Marianka has some understanding of the conventions of speaking and listening such as eye contact. She relies on pictorial clues to help her speech so would benefit from ensuring her learning tasks are context based.

### A spot of theory

*In their 2013–14 Cambridge Oracy Assessment Project, Neil Mercer along with Paul Warwick and Ayesha Ahmed identified four different aspects of communication which could be assessed: physical; linguistic; cognitive; and social and emotional communication.*

*The first aspect is focused on physical communication, which includes gesture, posture and eye contact. EAL learners would benefit greatly from establishing an early understanding of shared conventions of these elements of physical communication, especially as these reduce the need for linguistic skills from either the teacher or the learner, while simultaneously ensuring a relationship can develop.*

## Strategy: Opening up questions

You will recognise and value the difference between closed and open questions from your experiences as a teacher. When you work with EAL learners, it can be useful to reconsider your idea of open questioning to include using different tasks as a way to question learners to assess knowledge and understanding. Sometimes using questions and tasks focused on knowledge of language can support you to recognise what your EAL learners understand and what the next steps might be.

### 7. Listening

A different type of question to ask of your EAL learners involves asking them to listen. Discriminating different words from each other in a second language is challenging and should be carefully developed. In particular, new-to-English EAL learners benefit from being asked to listen carefully for vocabulary they have been learning. You might supply the learner with a checklist or table of language which you know has already been learned and ask the learner to tick off the words they hear. You can extend this by asking the EAL learner to try to write any other words they hear.

### 8. Learner-led questioning

After they have listened to the teacher, other adult or peer, you can encourage an EAL learner to ask what language was used. This can be directly linked to the English skills being developed in the individual and you can select when you might do this. Support the EAL learner with a checklist, for example of different word classes or different types of sentence. This would be useful to direct more advanced EAL learners. After listening, your EAL learner could be given the chance to ask about the language they heard: *Was it a noun? Did you use a command? Was that a dialect word?*

### 9. Enabling options

When you ask open questions, you are allowing all learners the opportunity to share and extend their thinking. Your EAL learners may need some extra scaffolding to facilitate this as they concentrate on ensuring they have the English vocabulary to match their ideas. Using talk time is one way to enable open answers, and you can also provide helpful tables and pictures which they might choose from when sharing their ideas. This added context can reduce the pressure to recall and develop English while also challenging the EAL learners to think about different ideas.

*Provide a checklist of different word classes for EAL learners*

To develop language alongside learning in other subjects, you might ask your EAL learner to keep a record of the English words they hear during shared teaching times. This is especially effective when teaching subjects which can be clearly supported with matching visuals on a word mat. Teaching more abstract concepts will be explored later in this book.

Your EAL learner is asked to mark on the table anything they hear as you, another adult or a peer is talking with them. The example table below could be used during a Key Stage 2 science lesson.

| skeleton | movement | human |
|----------|----------|-------|
| muscles | support | protection |

You can use this in a range of subject areas and might differentiate it through the addition of picture clues for new-to-English learners, and through the use of dual language vocabulary cards. You can offer challenge for more advanced EAL learners through the use of complete sentences or challenging vocabulary.

Note how use of a table or word mat can help you to scaffold learning of English and maximise learning opportunities as the learner has the chance to hear the word and to see the written form. Providing word mats further individualises the support offered to the EAL learner.

**A spot of theory**

*Generating questions to both stimulate and assess learning is part of your role as a teacher. Baumfield and Mroz (2002) looked more closely at questioning and suggested that when learners are given time to generate their own questions then this can impact on the development of independence, autonomy and understanding. For EAL learners to make progress, it is essential to help to develop independence as this will help learners to support themselves.*

## Strategy: Peer support

Dialogic teaching which encourages the use of discussion to explore ideas and develop understanding is part of the teaching practices of many educators today. Peer support can be used as an assessment strategy in which learners are able to offer each other suggestions on their work. Alongside this, peer support can be especially useful for new-to-English learners to practise their developing language skills. You can pair learners together who have similar abilities or organise learners by mixed ability, depending on the task. EAL learners will benefit from working with native English speakers and can also benefit from working with other EAL learners working at a similar language level.

## 10. All about us

Ask your learners to work together to share ideas and answer teacher-directed questions. Making this an expectation for any session can quickly involve EAL learners, even those who are new starters. You could set up reporter roles and key questions for your learners to create a class fact file. Whenever a new starter arrives, your class reporter can conduct an interview to find out some key information to share with you for the class fact file. When you have set an expectation that the learners will always share their findings, whether from interviews or paired discussions or any other talk opportunities, then EAL learners might feel encouraged from the example set by others.

## 11. Language partners

You can encourage new-to-English learners with support from peers who have the same mother tongue but are more advanced in their English language skills. Teachers can find the support from more advanced EAL learners invaluable. You might make use of language partners to help a new starter settle but more helpfully you can encourage extended conversations about particular topics. The advanced EAL learner benefits from the challenge of translating key aspects of the conversation into English and the new-to-English learner has the opportunity to be challenged in their mother tongue. Other learners might explain different word classes to their new-to-English peer, enabling them to practise their developing grasp of features such as nouns, verbs and adjectives as they help their peer.

## 12. Practice partners

If the new-to-English learner does not have the support from a peer who has the same mother tongue, peer support can still be useful. Other learners in the class can support a new-to-English learner to practise their language skills while they practise using the appropriate grammatical terminology. When you teach different grammatical structures, fronted adverbials for example, make it an expectation that your learners explain the language they are using. Practice partners can share their language skills even if they are at different levels; for example a learner working on complex sentences needs knowledge of simple sentences so can therefore help someone working at this level.

## Strategy in action

Here is a teacher who makes regular use of peer discussion to facilitate learning explaining the task. Note the combination of language and practice partner work.

" *Right, now that we have learned about different word classes I want you to explain your understanding to your partner.*

*Start with the expert interview approach: your partner needs to share everything they know. You can do this in any language to check your ideas first.*

*Then I want you to really think carefully and tweet what you know.*

*Yes, you can come up with the tweet together. But it must be only 140 characters... decide what you can explain most clearly...*

★ How might a new-to-English learner benefit from this?

★ Consider how a language partner task might be added to this.

★ How can 'tweeting' challenge more advanced EAL learners?

### A spot of theory

*When examining ways of fostering early language in 2001, Dickinson and Tabors identified the importance of offering varied opportunities to take part in extended conversations. Conversations at home and at school in their mother tongue is just as important for EAL learners as developing skills in English language. Ability in extended mother tongue conversations can be indicative of advanced cognitive skills, suggesting that as English talk skills develop then extended conversations may eventually follow.*

### Answers

☑ New-to-English learners have the opportunity to hear English used by more confident peers and to practise their use of spoken English within a fixed number of words in an activity like this.

☑ You can easily add a language partner element through asking for a tweet composed in the mother tongue. Translation can be readily tackled as the topic is fixed for the pair.

☑ More confident English speakers may find it challenging to explain their understanding in a limited number of words, therefore ensuring all learners are making progress.

**If you only try one thing from this chapter, try this***

Checklist

Use this to keep a record of what worked well for you and what didn't. A strategy that works with one learner or group of learners may not work so well with another. Keeping a checklist helps you to work out what factors or learner characteristics call for one approach rather than another. There's a line at the bottom for you to add your own most frequently used strategy, if it's not already included in the list.

| Strategy | Tried it with... | On...(date) | It worked | It didn't work | Worth trying again? |
|---|---|---|---|---|---|
| 1. Navigating the day | | | | | |
| 2. Survival language | | | | | |
| **3. Comprehensible cultural contexts*** | | | | | |
| 4. Practising vocabulary | | | | | |
| 5. Thinking and talking time | | | | | |
| 6. Pick up a sticky note | | | | | |
| 7. Listening | | | | | |
| 8. Learner-led questioning | | | | | |
| 9. Enabling options | | | | | |
| 10. All about us | | | | | |
| 11. Language partners | | | | | |
| 12. Practice partners | | | | | |
| Your own strategy? | | | | | |

# DAY 2: Strategies to develop reading and writing for EAL learners

## Cracking the code: teaching literacy skills

The language skills you develop through providing speaking and listening opportunities prove invaluable when developing literacy skills – reading and writing – with EAL learners. Here you will find strategies to help you teach EAL learners to read and write well. The strategies offer suggestions for providing effective classroom support such as reminders of grammatical rules alongside practical suggestions for teaching reading and writing within a multicultural classroom.

The chapter aims to outline some key principles for teaching reading and writing – such as using phonics – along with distinctive ideas for EAL learners. The chapter begins with simple ideas to prepare for teaching EAL learners, and importantly to help you recognise the challenges presented by the English language!

These strategies cover the teaching of reading and writing for EAL learners in any classroom.

* Keep challenges clear:
  1. A context question?
  2. Point out the problems!
  3. Vital vocabulary

* Teaching reading:
  4. Find time for phonics
  5. Is it English?
  6. Listen to learn
  7. Rainbow reading

* Teaching writing:
  8. Talk tennis
  9. Scribble and scribe
  10. Transformation tasks

## Strategy: Keep challenges clear

The English language can be a tricky thing to master. Take the word 'read' for example: in the middle of a book you *read*, and this *read* rhymes with *seed*. When you have finished the book, you can say you have *read it*, but this time *read* rhymes with *bed*. Confusing isn't it? While you cannot learn every language, you can learn in what ways English is unique, and make these really explicit for the EAL learners in your classroom. Encouraging EAL learners to develop and understand a wide range of vocabulary can help with both reading and writing. Supporting EAL learners to grasp English can include developing the classroom environment as well as using specific teaching approaches. The strategies here are intended to offer teachers support to address some of the key challenges faced by EAL learners as they develop reading and writing skills in the classroom.

### 1. A context question?

Grammatical rules can be very usefully learned in context by sharing examples from reading or by teaching particular rules before expecting learners to apply these in their own writing. For example, you might teach children how to use the imperative before they write a set of instructions. This is very good practice but in addition EAL learners can benefit from having explicit grammar instruction in order to understand the particular rules before applying these to their own writing. When you plan your English lessons, a guided group activity might focus on grammar so that EAL learners can have some further support within your planned lesson time. Alternatively, you could teach grammar lessons discretely. You might consider teaching the required grammar based on the needs of a genre or based on the learners' previous writing skills.

### 2. Point out the problems!

Spending a little time thinking about the function of the language to be used or read and the structure this might take and displaying these can help you to foresee any challenges for individual EAL learners. Classroom display spaces should be used to help your EAL learners to work independently. Displays of the common challenges can be referenced when EAL learners are reading or writing, and you should make it clear that the classroom is a place where they will be helped to practise and learn. Your language wall might include:

* rules and the exceptions to these;
* word order;
* pronunciation;
* synonyms;
* homophones;
* regional differences.

The precise content of your language wall display will depend on the age and stage of your EAL learners.

### 3. Vital vocabulary

Understanding vocabulary is central to being able to read and write well. Your EAL learners may have effective decoding and encoding skills for reading and writing but a wide vocabulary will help to ensure the EAL learners can understand what they are reading as well as selecting the most appropriate language choices for their writing. Collecting and classifying vocabulary is a vital strategy that can very easily be adapted for a whole class. Use books, online texts and any other sources such as newspapers and magazines to challenge EAL learners to collect new vocabulary to help develop their range. Your EAL learners could collect examples of a word class they have been learning about or different words for use in their own writing. You can start by directing the vocabulary search, and extend the task when needed by asking EAL learners to classify the collections themselves.

## Strategy in action

Grammatical rules, spelling rules and vocabulary can be taught discretely and in context. Victoria, a Year 3 teacher, has considered whether discrete or context-based teaching would be best for grammar and punctuation teaching for her EAL learners. Would you agree and teach these discretely or in context? Or would you prefer to use a range of approaches?

| Discrete teaching | Context-based teaching |
|---|---|
| • Spelling rules including forming nouns with suffixes like *−s*, *−es*, *−ful*, *−ness* and prefixes like *un−*, *dis−*, *super−*<br>• Reminders of co-ordinating conjunctions like *and*<br>• Homophones | • Punctuation reminders including full stops, apostrophes and commas<br>• Reminders of capital letters and separation of words with spaces<br>• Exploring word order<br>• Synonyms |

### A spot of theory

*In her book* Learning to Learn in a Second Language *(1993), Pauline Gibbons recommends that when you plan teaching ideas, you should consider the language you use carefully, thinking about the form this will take in a text, as well as the function of the words, sentences and paragraphs in the text. By thinking through what language is used and how before you start teaching, you may be able to predict what the challenges are, and identify which aspects of a particular text type need more attention. Considering the vocabulary carefully can also help you to direct EAL learners in collecting and classifying their own useful language lists.*

# Strategy: Teaching reading

Teaching someone to read is one of the most important things any teacher can do. As a teacher you should recognise that reading comprises two distinct aspects: word reading and comprehension. Being able to sound out the phonemes to read a word such as *c-a-t* and say words such as *said* from a flashcard out loud is the start; being able to understand what these words mean when matched to pictures helps to encourage reading comprehension; reading and appreciating words in a range of different contexts establishes understanding. The reading strategies here can be used alongside shared, guided and one-to-one reading. These practical suggestions should help EAL learners to develop word reading skills and to demonstrate their growing comprehension of the English language.

## 4. Find time for phonics

The opportunities you have to teach using systematic synthetic phonics (blending sounds to make a word) will vary greatly depending on the age of your learners. Primary school teachers have the advantage of utilising phonics regularly – at least in the Early Years Foundation Stage (EYFS) and Key Stage 1. The key to establishing an understanding of the sounds (phonemes) made by letters and combinations of letters (graphemes) is regular and consistent practice. Look to exploit all opportunities to make use of robotic-type speech to aid the important development of blending phonemes to read, and segmenting phonemes to spell. Dual language labels in the classroom can be presented a third way – as separate graphemes for example. As the EAL learners move around the learning spaces, taking a couple of extra moments to highlight phonemes – such as 'get your *c-oa-t*, *coat*' as you point to the word – is really useful to embed the skill of blending into everyday practice, particularly when working with older EAL learners in Key Stage 2 who might not have had the chance to pick up this reading approach in Key Stage 1.

## 5. Is it English?

Languages grow and develop all of the time – this is one of the most fun aspects of learning English at any level. Several English words originate from other languages, as you'll recognise from visits to restaurants and cafes. Exploring etymology is interesting and motivating for EAL learners, especially if learners find language from their home country and words used widely around the world in the books they read. To get started you can share vocabulary with groups and use dictionaries to explore definitions. Younger learners could be given words originating from other languages while older or more advanced learners can be challenged to find the origin themselves.

## 6. Listen to learn

Speaking and listening skills contribute greatly to making progress in reading. You can maximise opportunities for EAL learners to hear native speakers by recording key vocabulary or even a complete text so that learners can hear English when possible. This is more helpful than you might think. Alphabet systems may be the same, but this is not necessarily the case for pronunciation. Some language systems use equal stress for every syllable, while in English there are unstressed syllables and exceptions to watch out for! Think about the word *helped*. If you enunciate the ending then what normally sounds like **helpt** would become **help-ed**. Providing recordings of key or new vocabulary for a text can support EAL learners to develop their reading independently.

## 7. Rainbow reading

As well as the blending and word reading skills practised through teaching phonics, you need to support learners to develop comprehension skills. Rainbow reading can ensure inclusion is achieved, while at the same time giving appropriately challenging texts for different learners. By using different texts on the same theme, you can provide a group reading task which all learners can take part in. You can help EAL learners if you make use of the wide range of illustrated and picture books available for older readers. Moreover, you could make use of other graphic illustrations, photographs and paintings to cognitively challenge EAL learners as word reading skills develop.

## Strategy in action

To make use of *rainbow reading*, first organise the learners into smaller groups. Each member of the group has a different but appropriate text on the same theme (make it a rainbow by copying these onto different coloured paper!). Once each has been 'read' have a single list of questions for the group, carefully planned so that at least one question relates to each text, thereby ensuring all members are expected to closely read their given text.

In a Year 5 lesson on biographies for example, where the class is divided into groups of three, a more advanced EAL learner or native speaker might read an extract of a biography – such as the life of painter Henri Matisse. A less competent reader could read from an online biography – such as a museum entry – or from a fictionalised account of his life; a new-to-English EAL learner could be given an example of Matisse's artwork to closely examine. If there are questions related to each 'text' then the more competent learner cannot assume the lead, giving all learners the chance to succeed.

### A spot of theory

*Jim Cummins has written widely on supporting English language learning. He highlights the differences between conversational fluency and the proficiency of language required for academic success in his book from 2000:* Language, Power and Pedagogy. *These two areas are explained by Cummins as: BICS – basic interpersonal communication skills and CALP – cognitive academic language proficiency. EAL learners need time to develop in both areas and Cummins identifies the need to develop speaking and listening for reading and writing.*

# Strategy: Teaching writing

When you teach EAL learners to write or to improve their writing skills, you will benefit greatly from providing a rich context which can stimulate writing and about which your EAL learners can write. The aim of these strategies is to provide a toolkit for you to teach and improve writing practically and quickly, with the goal of providing context-based learning opportunities which can be easily changed, and eventually to move away from using a context. Though a rich context such as writing about a visit or about their lives really helps EAL learners, it is vital that they also move towards application of writing skills in different contexts and possibly out of context completely. If your EAL learners have confidence in the content from one particular genre, you can encourage writing of different genres by changing the purpose of the writing task. This way your EAL learners can make use of some of the key topic-related vocabulary which has already been learned, while further developing their writing skills.

## 8. Talk tennis

Generating ideas, formulating correct sentences and then writing these down legibly is potentially a lengthy thought process. For EAL learners to write in English, they will need to think of ideas in their home language and then work out the matching English. When you work with EAL learners, make talk for writing an expectation of the process, and ensure that the talk includes classifications of the language used, keeping this appropriate to their level. Talk tennis is an ideal way to support EAL learners to bounce ideas around with a partner. To ensure the EAL learners have a little thinking time, include an umpire – this might be you, another adult or one of their peers. The first player serves their word and when the umpire allows, the partner responds with another word. You can develop this by theme, such as story language to use, or by word class, such as adjectives or nouns.

## 9. Scribble and scribe

If you visit a nursery classroom you will no doubt spot writing opportunities everywhere. Young children are keen to 'have a go' and will happily read the marks they have made to you as a story, telephone message or shopping list for instance. Encouraging this sort of have-a-go approach can help EAL learners to build confidence in their writing skills. Listening as EAL learners talk, you might jot down the English words they use on a sticky note. This can reduce the pressure on EAL learners to write because they have you as a scribe. If you have well-established partners working in your classroom, make it standard practice for pairs to act as a scribe for each other's ideas. You might also use storyboards or another form of picture representation pre-writing. This again reduces the pressure to write, and provides a helpful reminder of the content.

Support for writing through scribbling and scribing also includes:

* story maps;
* counting words before writing and again to check;
* writing frames;
* word mats.

The tools you select will depend very much on the age and stage of the EAL learner but the goal is the same – developing learner independence and self-reliance for writing.

## 10. Transformation tasks

As the EAL learners improve their writing skills, you need to consider offering opportunities for writing tasks to be undertaken out of context. Asking learners to write out of context can obviously be used as an assessment tool. But it does not just have to be used to assess. Even more usefully, plan opportunities for EAL learners to use the toolkit of strategies already developing – talk partners, scribbles, scribes, rehearsal, and word counting then repeated checking – to facilitate demonstration of self-reliance and independence in writing. In a Year 5 history lesson for example, ask learners to write first person accounts such as diary entries of the particular topic being explored. While the content is known from history teaching, the learners will need to utilise skills learned in English lessons to complete the task well.

## Strategy in action

The more opportunities to practise and to record ideas, the more quickly EAL learners can embed their language and literacy skills. In the following table is a list of ideas generated by Key Stage 1 colleagues for exploring ideas, recording plans and text transformation based on the traditional tale *The Three Little Pigs*.

| Talking tasks | Scribbling tasks | Transformation tasks |
|---|---|---|
| *Noun tennis* – what could the house be made from?<br><br>*Adjective tennis* – other words for big | Draw the house for the pigs<br><br>Draw a map of the journey between the houses<br><br>Paired story map<br><br>Teacher scribe retelling | Instructions for building a house<br><br>Labels for the features of a house<br><br>Postcard from the wolf or the pigs |

### A spot of theory

*In her 2014 study 'Drawing to Support Language Development in English Language Learners', Misty Adoniou examined and presented the importance of both experience and keeping a record to support writing. She describes how the EAL learners who drew pictures of the baking task as they experienced it were able to write much more than those who baked but relied on memory for writing. This reminds us of the value of something as simple as a jotter and some scribbles to stimulate writing success.*

**Checklist**

Use this to keep a record of what worked well for you and what didn't. A strategy that works with one learner or group of learners may not work so well with another. Keeping a checklist helps you to work out what factors or learner characteristics call for one approach rather than another. There's a line at the bottom for you to add your own most frequently used strategy, if it's not already included in the list.

| Strategy | Tried it with... | On...(date) | It worked | It didn't work | Worth trying again? |
|---|---|---|---|---|---|
| 1. A context question? | | | | | |
| 2. Point out the problems! | | | | | |
| 3. Vital vocabulary | | | | | |
| 4. Find time for phonics | | | | | |
| 5. Is it English? | | | | | |
| 6. Listen to learn | | | | | |
| **7. Rainbow reading*** | | | | | |
| 8. Talk tennis | | | | | |
| 9. Scribble and scribe | | | | | |
| 10. Transformation tasks | | | | | |
| Your own strategy? | | | | | |

## Today's strategies

## Language learning beyond literacy lessons

When you teach in a primary school you need to have a good understanding of subject knowledge across all curriculum subjects. Language and literacy skills are of course essential across the curriculum because as teachers you will be using language all of the time. Learners will listen to new ideas, talk about their understanding and share answers. In some subjects like history or geography, learners might read to develop their subject knowledge and in turn might write to illustrate this. This can be more complicated for an EAL learner since they will be developing their understanding of a subject in English – a language different from their mother tongue. To help your learners manage the language demands across the curriculum, you need to ensure that you plan opportunities to introduce subject-specific language and to apply this. It is important to make the language teaching explicit for EAL learners because the language used for a particular function (purpose) might change depending on the subject-specific language needs. Think about how language is used in different curriculum areas and provide explicit signposts to this for your EAL learners. For example, consider if they are using language to explain, describe, report or compare. In this chapter for Day 3 language-focused ideas are presented.

The suggested strategies and resource ideas included here aim to show how effective language and literacy ideas can be adapted for other curriculum areas. It can be really helpful to have resources which you can rely on and reuse for different purposes. When you are planning lessons and activities to support and develop EAL learners and you know that a resource can be used in several ways then this will ease your workload. Moreover, in the same way that developing strategies for partner work can become embedded in learning, so too can the use of different resources, which again aids independence and self-reliance – essential for EAL learner success.

- Subject-specific language needs:
  1. Language detectives
  2. Content for concepts
  3. Functional frames
  4. Language packs

- Classroom resources and teaching ideas:
  5. Paired problem solving
  6. Sequencing tasks
  7. Visual texts

- Barrier games – top timesavers!
  8. Describing games
  9. Mapping games
  10. Use cloze to close the gap

# Strategy: Subject-specific language needs

Identifying the key vocabulary for a specific subject is one of the most helpful ways you can provide support for your EAL learners. Lists of new vocabulary for a subject can be quite common when working with younger learners, but perhaps if you work in secondary or further education you might not be used to this. Think about the French, German or Spanish lessons you might have had at school. Did you learn new vocabulary for the different themes – like going to the cafe or at the train station? Vocabulary linked to subject content, themes and concepts is a key aspect of English language learning for EAL learners but needs to be developed alongside an understanding of the form and function of the language. The ideas in this section are aimed at supporting your ideas for planning so that your EAL learners are given more opportunities to develop self-reliance and to increase their independence so that you can work with all learners in the classroom effectively.

## 1. Language detectives

Whatever the subject is, aim to make sure you include a language-based objective too. When planning lessons for any classes which include EAL learners, include an activity which will help learners to develop and extend their vocabulary. You can give EAL learners word mats or lists of new vocabulary but even better is to encourage learners to look for the language themselves. There are a number of different ways of extending this 'magpie' technique. For new-to-English learners start with looking for words which begin with the same letter or letters. You can extend the challenge of this language detective work by asking more advanced EAL learners to collect vocabulary linked to a word class or theme. A further extension could be to ask for the collected vocabulary to be classified, for example into nouns, verbs and adjectives.

## 2. Content for concepts

No doubt there will be new concepts to learn for everyone in your class but you need to consider specific content words which you might assume other learners fluent in English would know. To prepare for this, strip the subject back to basics and build from this. Present some specific content words with your class at the start of a lesson – up to five words would be enough – and challenge pairs to share definitions, starting from the basics. This gives all learners the chance to quickly refresh their knowledge and understanding and offers you the chance to assess language needs directly. Challenge learners to keep a tally of the number of times they hear these words used.

## 3. Functional frames

If you plan writing tasks to record understanding across the curriculum, think carefully about the function of the language that will be used. You can use writing frames to indicate to EAL learners how words might change depending on their purpose in the writing. A writing frame has a clear layout using text boxes for each section of a particular written form. You can use headings or sentence starters for each section of the writing frame – think about the layout of a recipe for instance. Science is a very clear example of when the function of the language used needs to be clearly understood. The function of language in science might be to predict, explain and report, which might be written as an experiment. In this subject, EAL learners will experience verbs functioning in the future, present and past tense. And this could be the same verb as you can see from the headings in the following list.

- Prediction: We predict the ice cube *will melt* in the sun.
- Observations: The ice cube is *melting*.
- What happened: In the sun, the ice cube *melted*.

To really help EAL learners understand the writing frame, you can use pictures or diagrams as another clue.

## 4. Language packs

Preparing language packs for your subject can really help your EAL learners as well as easing your workload. Use the content words and the language you identified in your planning to create packs linked to learning objectives, which can be provided to help EAL learners over a sequence of lessons on a theme or during a topic; you can adapt this to meet your planning needs. Just like a word bank is useful for a literacy lesson, your language pack could be developed for all subjects rather than just English. Use pictures to make the language understandable too. Your EAL learners will of course be at different stages and have different language needs so you can differentiate the language in the packs – perhaps using a range of colours. If you create packs linked to a theme or topic you can reuse these language packs. Even if your lesson activity changes – as you develop the range of strategies in your personal 'toolkit' or bank of favourite and effective strategies – the language packs will still be relevant and useful for your EAL learners.

### Strategy in action

Key Stage 2 teacher Ray created a language pack for the EAL learners in his Year 3 class. After his NQT year he moved into Year 4. He was able to use the language pack again for new starters in his class who had EAL and to consolidate language knowledge for more established EAL learners.

Ray made packs for the language used in different subjects. Here is an example of the mathematics language and relevant symbols.

| addition | subtraction | multiplication | division |
|----------|-------------|----------------|----------|
| + | − | × | ÷ |
| add | minus | times | share by |
| plus | takeaway | | split |
| increase | decrease | | |

### A spot of theory

*Pauline Gibbons, an Australian-based education consultant and recognised expert on EAL and multicultural teaching, emphasises the importance of developing and supporting English in all areas of the curriculum. She suggests offering opportunities for EAL learners to report back on their learning – a key opportunity to practise the language! You can read more in her book:* Learning to Learn in a Second Language *(1993).*

# Strategy: Classroom resources and teaching ideas

Do you have favourite resources, lesson ideas and 'go to' strategies which have proven successful in both engaging the class and ensuring progress in learning? Armed with an understanding of the language needs of the subject, you can continue to use your favourite strategies. Useful tried and tested approaches for EAL learners which could be added to your repertoire are outlined here. You may even choose to select one strategy and adapt this for different subjects to allow EAL learners to embed this learning approach. Establishing expectations and rules for paired and group talk help ensure that EAL learners know they should make contributions in activities like this.

## 5. Paired problem solving

This activity is particularly useful in a mathematics or science lesson but could be adapted for any curriculum area which includes problem-solving objectives, such as outdoor and adventurous activities in PE or selecting the best vegetables to use to make instruments in Key Stage 2 design technology lessons! Set a number of problems for your class – a minimum of two different problems would be needed. This simple activity involves pairs discussing how they would solve the problem and sharing this solution with other pairs in the class. You might encourage note-taking or recording devices if you are limited in how many learners you can observe (and therefore assess) during the lesson. Providing language packs and appropriate word banks for EAL learners will further develop the goal of independent and self-reliant learning.

## 6. Sequencing tasks

Sequencing tasks can include retelling a story – as you might find in an English lesson. This activity is a useful way for learners to demonstrate their knowledge of any key learning which includes a particular order such as life cycles in science, dates and times in mathematics or historical timelines. EAL learners benefit from being given pictures to sequence; you can extend and challenge with written text as and when your learners are ready. To encourage more use of dialogue, you could split pictures among a group and ask each member to describe their picture – using a given word list – before the group agree together on a sequence. Remember that not all languages write scripts from left to right so you might need to point out this direction to your EAL learners.

## 7. Visual texts

When working with EAL learners it is really useful to be flexible in your definition of a text. For instance, if you are teaching about the lives of significant individuals such as Neil Armstrong and the moon landing in history in Key Stage 1 then photographs could be useful 'texts' from which learners can develop an understanding of significant events without needing a high level of reading skills. Paintings, photographs and films can be used in other curriculum areas too – for example, you could use a landscape painting of an area to explore changes in land use in geography lessons and films of different dance styles could be shared via tablets during lessons for learners to refer to, rather than sharing text-based instructions.

Here is a list of three key activities from a teacher who decided to utilise sequencing tasks across several subjects with a Year 6 class. Which subjects might these be adapted for?

- planning ideas using a flow chart;
- reordering texts;
- timelines.

*Photographs can be useful 'texts' from which learners can develop an understanding of significant events.*

## Answers

- ☑ Flow charts work well in any subject where plans need to be structured or an order decided. This would include, for example, English, maths, and science.
- ☑ Reordering a text would be useful in history or geography when cause and effect might be explored.
- ☑ Other than history, timelines can work very well to plot events, for example as a sequence of steps in decision making in PE or PSHE.

## Strategy: Barrier games — top timesavers!

Aimed at pairs, barrier games can be any activity or game requiring clear communication, and using a barrier to ensure this is verbal rather than visual communication. This might involve asking questions to solve a problem, or relaying information to explain a solution. To set up this activity you need to create a form of 'barrier' — a large piece of card folded so it stands up usually works. Alternatively, you might ask pairs to work back-to-back if that works for the task. When you set up your barriers you might display written and pictorial clues guiding players to follow certain communication rules in the game, such as speak clearly and ask the speaker to repeat themselves, plus a list of useful questions.

These games can be used for a wide variety of subjects from using directional language in mathematics to drawing locations correctly on maps in geography to using appropriate time connectives to sequence historical events. After the activity is complete the pair should compare their responses. You can make this as competitive as you want but the goal is for your EAL learners to have the opportunity to communicate using subject-specific language, and for you to have a resource and strategy that can be adapted and used in different ways over and over again.

## 8. Describing games

You can make common games like odd one out, matching games or bingo more challenging with a barrier. For odd one out, give the pair slightly different pictures — including written text if EAL learners are ready — with the challenge to describe their pictures and identify what the differences are. Provide a barrier between games where players need to find matching pairs to ensure language use is expected. Word banks can be helpful for this activity. This can link to any curriculum area and focus on a specific subject content shared with the learners.

## 9. Mapping games

Give pairs the task of directing each other through a map. This is an excellent opportunity for the partners to practise instructional and directional language as well as time or sequential connectives. There is a chance for learners to practise content words with a map-based barrier game if you task the learners with navigating through particular features found within a specific theme. This is not restricted to geography as you might provide a map or plan of a museum and ask pairs to guide each other past particular exhibits which have formed part of their recent history learning for instance.

## 10. Use cloze to close the gap

Cloze procedure activities involve learners working out the missing words from a passage or set of sentences. To use cloze as a barrier game give each pair a text. The overall text should be the same but each partner has different missing words. Through understanding the language needs of your EAL learners, you can carefully decide which words to hide. If you are developing an understanding of verbs for EAL learners then you might remove these for one partner while focusing on subject-specific vocabulary for the other partner. The aim is for the pairs to work out the missing words from their text from listening to each other and discussing the gaps. Keeping the barrier in place can encourage attempts at writing the missing vocabulary too. You might support EAL learners by providing a list of words to select from but keep some challenge by including red herrings in this too.

After introducing the class to different artworks in Year 4, the teacher plans opportunities for the learners to review their understanding of these through a barrier game to match descriptions and paintings. One of the learners is presented with a single painting; the other has a range of paintings from the two movements. The teacher includes a list of subject-specific vocabulary for both learners linked to art elements including colour, shape and line. Because the EAL learner is fairly new to English, the teacher includes picture clues with the vocabulary list to help. A recording device is also offered so that the EAL learner can recap the description if needed. The learner with the single painting describes this and the partner listens, asks questions and aims to identify the painting from the range they have been given. This task is repeated using a different painting for the partner to describe.

- Do you think the recording device would be helpful?

- Would it be more appropriate for the EAL learner to have the single picture first or second?

**A spot of theory**

*Teaching EAL learners by using games can reflect more recent emphasis on learning through doing and engaging in active and multisensory experiences. Rae Pica highlights this in her work on active learning (see further reading).*

Answers

☑ The recording device might be more helpful in this case so that the EAL learner can clarify the description and to check which words were understood or missed when the answer was revealed. It is better to offer this as an option rather than an expectation as the EAL learner may be embarrassed or simply prefer to practise asking clarifying questions.

☑ Giving the EAL learner the chance to describe a painting second would be beneficial because they would have the opportunity to hear descriptive language modelled from their partner.

**If you only try one thing from this chapter, try this\***

Use this to keep a record of what worked well for you and what didn't. A strategy that works with one learner or group of learners may not work so well with another. Keeping a checklist helps you to work out what factors or learner characteristics call for one approach rather than another. There's a line at the bottom for you to add your own most frequently used strategy, if it's not already included in the list.

| Strategy | Tried it with... | On...(date) | It worked | It didn't work | Worth trying again? |
|---|---|---|---|---|---|
| 1. Language detectives | | | | | |
| 2. Content for concepts | | | | | |
| 3. Functional frames | | | | | |
| 4. Language packs | | | | | |
| 5. Paired problem solving | | | | | |
| 6. Sequencing tasks | | | | | |
| 7. Visual texts | | | | | |
| **8. Describing games\*** | | | | | |
| 9. Mapping games | | | | | |
| 10. Use cloze to close the gap | | | | | |
| Your own strategy? | | | | | |

## Differentiating and planning for EAL learners

Imagine you are planning your week's lessons for your different classes or subjects. How do you apply differentiation in these lessons? Every learning setting is different – you might stream your learners by ability, work with mixed ability groups or differentiate differently for different purposes. When you work with EAL learners it is important to think about whether you need to consider any further means of differentiation to ensure that all learners can make progress. There are various strategies which you might use to help EAL learners to achieve the goal of the particular lesson. Whether you are a more experienced teacher or an NQT developing your teaching skill set, it is worth thinking about adding an appropriate extra layer of differentiation to your lesson in order to support success, aid learning and facilitate independence and self-reliance in your EAL learners. As you already no doubt know, to plan effectively it is important that you understand the different needs of all learners in your class.

There is no single route to navigate effective differentiation for your EAL learners but Day 4 provides you with a range of strategies which can aid your planning and preparation. You may find different strategies work better for different classes of learners or for different subjects. It is worth flipping back over suggested strategies and resources included in previous sections too. Keep in mind what resources you might need and what you already have as you explore this chapter to help you differentiate in your planning. The chapter begins with classroom management to help you to rethink the organisation of your teaching time during lessons. Finally, there are some suggestions to help you ensure your EAL learners are effectively challenged – which can be very useful for more advanced bilinguals.

Before you do start planning, it is important to ensure that you gather as much information about your EAL learners as possible to provide appropriate support for language development needs but also to support and challenge EAL learners correctly in other subjects. Think about questions like:

- What, if any, schooling have they had in their mother tongue?
- How competently do they speak, read or write in their mother tongue?
- How well can they complete mathematics calculations?

Do they demonstrate skills in practical subjects (for example, art, DT, PE)? EAL learners must be given appropriately challenging work in subjects such as mathematics, art and DT which are less demanding in relation to language.

### Today's strategies

- Classroom management:
  1. Classroom needs
  2. To share or not to share?
  3. Signposts

- Differentiation strategies:
  4. Questions
  5. Tasks
  6. Time

- Keep challenge in check:
  7. Variety packs
  8. Chatter books

# Strategy: Classroom management

When you plan individual lessons, think about how you might indicate to learners what the expectation is during different parts of a lesson. There are times when you want learners to listen as you teach new concepts or model examples, times when you expect partner talk and times when you will expect responses to questions. Consider the timings of each part of the lesson, how you will make the expectations of each section clear to EAL learners and how you will organise the classroom space to facilitate effective talk strategies as well as where visual reminders and rules can be best displayed. Grouping tables to encourage interaction and having accessible materials such as word banks and recording devices establishes effective ways of working. Giving your EAL learners clear guidance on the use of the supporting resources as well as how to interact in a group further helps you and your learners to succeed in a diverse classroom. The following suggested strategies could further support your classroom management to maximise learning. As teachers, it is very helpful to have a well-managed and well-resourced classroom. This is even more important if you are teaching a class with multiple languages. If there are several learners with the same mother tongue they can help each other, and should be encouraged to do so.

## 1. Classroom needs

A simple but effective approach to implement when getting to grips with the diverse language needs of EAL learners in your class is to consider how useful your environment is. Think about the following questions when you are planning:

* Does the layout of your tables allow for group work?
* Are the resources readily available?
* Is there space for resources on tables?
* Are the displays helpful?
* Do displays help scaffold language?
* Are visual clues and reminders used?
* Do learners know expectations of working (eg sharing ideas and talking together)?

## 2. To share or not to share?

You might be familiar with a planning model which follows a pattern like this:

* shared teaching
* group or independent work
* plenary

Typically the whole class would work together at the start and the end of the lesson. Think about how useful this is for your EAL learners. There might be some EAL learners who are missing key learning opportunities because of their language needs. Instead of whole class teaching, try working with smaller groups from the outset. Your planning model would then be:

* share with group 1 / group 2 independent
* swap groups
* plenary

You can provide tasks which some groups can explore independently – such as revisiting corrections from a previous day – while you teach one group, and then swap the groups round. This way you can maximise the teaching time for your EAL learners and avoid leaving these learners floundering because of the language challenge they face.

## 3. Signposts

EAL learners may need time to process a response in their native language and to translate this to comprehensible English output. You can successfully give EAL learners this processing time by signposting when you will be asking questions and by giving learners thinking time to prepare answers to more open questions. Tell your class that in five minutes you will be asking questions; hand out some sentence starts or key vocabulary and explain that this will help them in ten minutes when they have to share responses; or use a timer to indicate the different parts of your lesson to your EAL learners. Choose what works best for you but try giving your EAL learners a little prompting about the expectations at different times in a lesson to see if this helps.

### Strategy in action

✱ Compare the ways these two Year 4 teachers signpost the direction of the learning in lessons. How do you think EAL learners would manage? What messages are the teachers giving?

| Teacher A | Teacher B |
|---|---|
| *Okay, so today we are learning to use the grid method for multiplication.* | *Okay, so we are learning the grid method today. Let's practise the 8 × table first.* |
| *We'll start with five minutes of practising our 8 × table, then we'll work in talk pairs to use the grid method for ten minutes – and then you will be working out some questions independently. Is that okay?* | *Maroš and Marianka, don't worry I'll come to you in a minute. Just listen for now.* |
| *Right, Sami, can you see our timer? Five minutes first, then talk time. Tomaš the first number is 8, what is next?* | *Okay, so now everybody look at the board at the grid. I'll show you how to do one example… now use your whiteboard to try to solve the next one…* |
| *Here's a number square for everyone, look for the pattern for the 8 × table if you need it. Ready?* | *Matthew, what answer did you get? Can you explain?* |
| | *Good, now time to work on some examples at your tables.* |
| | *Maroš and Marianka, I'm ready.* |

Both teachers show awareness of the EAL learners but Teacher A ensures active participation.

## Answers

☑ Both teachers do articulate stages of the lesson, which is helpful for EAL learners.

☑ Teacher A sets clear timescales and clear outlines for how the learners will work. This indicates to EAL learners what they should do in each section.

☑ Teacher B does indicate to EAL learners Maroš and Marianka that they will get attention, but the message could suggest that they do not need to listen yet, perhaps isolating them from the rest of the class.

☑ Teacher A clearly has high expectations and has planned opportunities to include all learners.

# Strategy: Differentiation strategies

Learners' abilities need to be considered in your planning as you will no doubt know. Effective teachers will think about how to further differentiate beyond grouping similar ability learners together and think about how to offer support for smaller groups or individuals. Typically, differentiation might be by support or by outcome. Support can include teachers or other adults (see Day 5). It can also include the resources, some of which have been highlighted in other chapters, which you use to enable your EAL learners to complete a particular task. Differentiation by outcome has some benefits for EAL learners, particularly if you want to assess written outcomes, but there are other useful strategies presented here which can support EAL learners to fully engage with learning objectives set for the class as a whole, in order to help them make progress and become more independent.

## 4. Questions

You will be familiar with open and closed questions, remembering that an open question is designed to elicit an extended response or explanation while a closed question needs only a brief answer. In teacher training you might be advised to offer more open questions to allow learners to articulate their thoughts. When meeting the needs of EAL learners you should consider including *structured closed questions* to encourage EAL learners to demonstrate the progress they are making with learning. This is helpful because your EAL learners will be able to focus on a single answer rather than having to focus on working out possible solutions or explaining these – which would be useful for some of your learners. In mathematics for example you might give examples of calculations and ask EAL learners to indicate if these are right or wrong. If an answer is incorrect, move on

to partner problem solving – where two learners work together to find a solution – rather than asking individuals to explain how it might be solved.

## 5. Tasks

In mathematics you can differentiate for EAL learners with calculations which are less demanding in terms of use of English. In other subjects you should consider two aspects in particular:

* context;
* language

If you are working with EAL learners who are new to English, or when you introduce a new concept or topic, you should ensure that the learning is presented within a clear context. The context could be anything from a practical experience in geography, science, DT or PE which EAL learners write about, to providing images as a stimulus for writing stories or gathering historical information from photographic secondary sources. A visual stimulus can spur on language development, which is essential for EAL learners. Moreover, you can plan to ask questions about the language used, which further integrates language into the curriculum.

## 6. Time

When planning tasks for your EAL learners you might consider using time as a strategy. Rather than expecting less content – for instance a shorter piece of writing – you could plan for the learning activity to be completed over a sequence of lessons, thus allowing more time for it. Your EAL learners often have complex demands placed on them during lessons as they have to translate thinking into English to complete the learning task.

Learning tasks should be cognitively challenging for all learners so extra time could be planned to allow EAL learners to meet this two-fold challenge. Extra thinking time might be added to other parts of your lessons to give more time for paired talk and to answer questions. It is natural to worry about giving learners extra time. However, as long as the task includes appropriate challenge then it is reasonable to recognise and plan for the valuable time EAL learners will spend translating thoughts, ideas and understanding into English. You will be meeting their specific need. This, after all, is what differentiation is about.

**A spot of theory**

*In her book* Scaffolding Language, Scaffolding Learning: Teaching Second Language Learners in the Mainstream Classroom *(2002), Pauline Gibbons emphasises the role of talk in creating effective opportunities for successful EAL learners in the classroom. Learning can be maximised through effectively scaffolded tasks combined with planned opportunities to talk. Interaction through talk is useful in enabling all learners to think out loud, and for EAL learners this offers a further opportunity to practise developing language skills.*

**Strategy in action**

This extract from a plan shows a teacher who has considered more detailed language needs of the task. The teacher recognises that 'comparative language' might need some further explanation for EAL learners, so questions the class and is prepared to move from simple to more complicated comparisons. In the final column the teacher highlights the most appropriate differentiation approach to take.

| Learning objective/s | Language focus | Task and time | Focused language questions | Key resources | Key differentiation approaches |
|---|---|---|---|---|---|
| Analyse performances (Key Stage 2 dance) | Comparative language (from **good, better, best** to using sentence starts like **'on the other hand…'**) and past tense (plus general vocabulary) | Small groups perform planned dances<br><br>Record performances<br><br>Feedback to teacher<br><br>x 4 sessions | *Can you describe the movements seen?*<br><br>*When you use comparative language what should you be doing?*<br><br>*What does the past tense indicate?* | Tablets<br><br>Word mats<br><br>Sentence starters<br><br>Comparative phrases<br><br>Question prompts | By questioning<br><br>By task<br><br>By outcome<br><br>By support |

## Strategy: Keep challenge in check

Careful planning and considering a range of differentiation approaches can help you to effectively teach and support your EAL learners. It is important to keep focused on challenging EAL learners appropriately as some will pick up language more rapidly than others. Even in classes with a group of EAL learners with the same mother tongue, the learners will be at different stages in their grasp of English. Skills in other areas can be used as a scaffold for language development through the integration of appropriate language into other subjects but it is important to keep challenging the learners and to continue to develop language across all curriculum areas.

## 7. Variety packs

When planning for English language development in EAL learners, consider how the language needed can be extended so that EAL learners express themselves in more complex ways. If they master one correct way of expressing their thoughts or understanding then they might be tempted to continue with this tried and tested format. Instead, aim to encourage learners to explore a range of ways to say the same thing – even across the curriculum. For example, using *because* in science to explain cause and effect is correct, but there are other options. What about:

- *as a result of*
- *since*
- *so*
- *leading to*

Create your own variety packs of different language with boxes or baskets of the synonyms which EAL learners can access and use in their own spoken and written work.

## 8. Chatter books

To ensure that appropriate challenge and expectations are established for the range of EAL learners, using chatter books – a notepad for instance – can be useful to allow learners to jot down ideas after talking and listening to the teacher or their classmates. The notepad can be written in or drawn in by your EAL learners at the beginning of your lesson or the end of the day for instance. This gives all learners the chance to grow in confidence using marks to convey meaning. Providing individual chatter books gives all learners the chance to demonstrate their understanding or show their ideas by outcome. Links with particular subjects can be made by setting tasks such as: 'Tell me everything you know about...' or having a set of interview-style questions to lead the conversation, such as asking the learner to explain how they have tackled a mathematical problem or science experiment.

Compare the approaches taken by these two teachers to challenge EAL learners in their classes. Both are using challenging activities but in different ways.

| Teacher A | Teacher B |
|---|---|
| • Using recording devices to practise | • Listening to role models of English |
| • Audio books with matching vocabulary | • Paired talk |
| • Word wall, baskets and boxes | • Personal jotters |

Teacher A expects active learning from the outset, aiming not to miss any opportunities to facilitate progress.

Teacher B does use inclusive practice and the approach might benefit an anxious new-to-English learner during a silent period when they might try to quietly observe new surroundings.

The talk and jotters can help with practising and ensuring challenge is expected. There are different but equally effective ways of working with EAL learners.

Look at the displays in English lessons and use similar visual reminders to help with language needs of EAL learners in other subjects.

Think about being flexible with home language groupings sometimes. Encouraging English is excellent but can be exhausting, especially for new-to-English EAL learners. Allowing some home language talk can give these learners a break and time to focus on the particular subject.

**A spot of theory**

*Toronto-based academic Jim Cummins has researched second language acquisition extensively and explores the impact of barriers other than language such as socio-economic factors. Cummins found that it can take up to seven years to develop academic proficiency in a second language while conversational fluency might be achieved in around two years. You can explore this further in Cummins' influential book* Language, Power and Pedagogy: Bilingual Children in the Crossfire *(2000).*

Use this to keep a record of what worked well for you and what didn't. A strategy that works with one learner or group of learners may not work so well with another. Keeping a checklist helps you to work out what factors or learner characteristics call for one approach rather than another. There's a line at the bottom for you to add your own most frequently used strategy, if it's not already included in the list.

| Strategy | Tried it with... | On...(date) | It worked | It didn't work | Worth trying again? |
|---|---|---|---|---|---|
| 1. Classroom needs | | | | | |
| **2. To share or not to share?*** | | | | | |
| 3. Signposts | | | | | |
| 4. Questions | | | | | |
| 5. Tasks | | | | | |
| 6. Time | | | | | |
| 7. Variety packs | | | | | |
| 8. Chatter books | | | | | |
| Your own strategy? | | | | | |

## Supporting EAL learners in the classroom and beyond

Teachers often work alongside other adults to support and provide opportunities for learners. The support might be from nursery nurses, teaching assistants, students or volunteers from the local community and beyond. Whoever provides support in your classroom, it is important to consider how other adults can be best deployed to maximise progress for EAL learners. Today, on Day 5, ideas are presented which will help you to work alongside other adults to plan for and teach EAL learners within the classroom. Valuing the ideas, experience and input of other adults can help you to optimise learning and progress for EAL learners, as well as establishing supportive professional relationships which can help in your busy day-to-day teaching life. Even more importantly, you need to work with the other adults in your class with shared goals and expectations for your EAL learners. Make sure that you spend time planning with the other adults who will work with the EAL learners so that the developing English language skills can be targeted and monitored. Working closely together can also help you to quickly establish which strategies are effective for different groups in your class.

**Today's strategies**

* Planning with support staff:
  1. Setting SMART targets
  2. Focus on independent learning
  3. Language expectations: reframing questions and comments
* Working wisely:
  4. Pre-teaching
  5. Team teaching
  6. Post teaching
* Sharing success:
  7. Sticky situations
  8. Catch the overlap
  9. Keeping a record

---

## Strategy: Planning with support staff

As effective teachers know, planning can be made more effective by working with classroom colleagues to generate and share ideas. If you have EAL learners in your classroom, you should take time to plan with support staff to ensure that every opportunity is taken for EAL learners to make progress in their grasp of English. Planning is a collaborative process: you can share ideas with colleagues and gather other observations of learners' strengths and challenges. You can work together to set targets for EAL learners, discuss language and learning needs and develop strategies to foster independence.

### 1. Setting SMART targets

EAL learners who are new to English will make rapid progress as they develop language skills. Setting academic language targets works best if these are smart: Specific, Measurable, Achievable, Realistic and Time-bound (SMART). EAL learners might develop some language skills very quickly to aid social survival, but academic language skills, particularly in written language, take more time. By working with support staff, you can consider what language is needed to make progress in a particular subject or lesson and then break this into smaller, achievable targets. General targets might include:

- listening to and repeating sets of instructions;
- learning and using key questions;
- reading and writing new vocabulary.

With support staff – and ideally with EAL learners too – set a time frame for achieving targets, followed by revised targets and checks of embedded learning.

### 2. Focus on independent learning

Independence is central to the distinct pedagogy for EAL learners. Work with support staff to agree on the most appropriate independent approaches for each particular subject area or task. You can ask support staff to spend some time with EAL learners to model how they might help themselves in order to develop self-correcting strategies or if a task is challenging. Remind learners to blend phonemes to tackle new words in reading tasks; model segmenting for spelling before writing and indicate which display or working wall will be most useful for the task in hand to develop self-reliance. A focus on independent skills can also reinforce other learning. For instance, modelling how to find words in a dictionary or on a word mat can also reinforce awareness of the alphabet.

### 3. Language expectations: reframing questions and comments

As a teacher you will work diligently to explore effective and appropriate pedagogies to scaffold learners. Language plays a central role in this as you consider how to explain tasks and expectations to your learners. All learners may need concepts repeated or explained differently from time to time, and all benefit from articulating their understanding. In the classroom you outline tasks and model examples, sometimes rephrasing if it becomes clear that learners are uncertain. When working with EAL learners, this can be a very useful opportunity to expand individual language skills, especially if everyone has similar expectations. It can be really helpful for EAL learners to hear their use of English repeated back to them. If they ask questions to clarify their understanding, or offer answers, take the time to repeat this back, subtly correcting errors as you do this. Rather than demotivating learners by highlighting the mistakes, you can simply model the Standard English response using positive reinforcement and correction.

Read this example from a Year 3 classroom during a practical design technology lesson. Tomas is from Slovakia and moved with his family who are migrant workers, starting school in Year 2. The learners are making models of bridges supported by a classroom assistant who has demonstrated how to use the different materials and is now observing.

Classroom assistant: *That looks like a strong bridge – how will you test it?*

Tomas: *I put toy car on it.*

Classroom assistant: *Good idea. So you <u>will</u> put <u>the</u> toy car on it?*

Tomas: *Yes, I <u>will</u> put toy car on it.*

Classroom assistant: *That is a good idea. I wonder what will happen when you put <u>the</u> toy car on the bridge. What will happen to <u>the car</u> Tomas?*

Tomas: *<u>The car</u> will stay.*

### A spot of theory

*In his work on* Visible Learning *(2008), John Hattie highlights the value of seeing and understanding learning through the eyes of the learner. When you are able to see teaching and learning through the eyes of the learner, you can support, develop and strengthen learning opportunities more readily as you start to understand how learners are navigating through their study. In the case of EAL learners, setting and celebrating targets which link to their application of rapidly developing English skills provides evidence of clearly visible learning.*

In this short exchange the classroom assistant carefully facilitates Tomas's use of determiners through repetition and praise. Rather than halting the exchange, the classroom assistant simply repeats Tomas's sentences with slight alterations (as underlined), which Tomas incorporates in his own language use.

*Tomas explains what he is doing to the classroom assistant.*

The car will stay on the bridge.

# Strategy: Working wisely

Whole class teaching times can be really valuable, especially for sharing general content and modelling strategies which you want all learners to use. Group work can offer you an opportunity to support less confident learners, as well as to assess and monitor the needs of the EAL learners. Encouraging group work can help develop independence from the teacher by encouraging learners to rely on each other. As teachers, you or other adults you work with can also make use of one-to-one opportunities to give EAL learners full attention. Careful lesson planning helps to facilitate this.

## 4. Pre-teaching

Pre-teaching opportunities work best with individuals or small groups with similar language or learning needs. If you have a large number of EAL learners in your class, think carefully about who has similar needs so that you can ensure appropriate support is offered. Learners can be supported with vocabulary development, which may include practising word reading skills, exploring definitions to aid understanding and introducing EAL learners to new subject-specific vocabulary. Pre-teaching opportunities may also be used to model strategies which EAL learners could use to develop independence and to discover how they can help themselves. This might include practising key questions which can be used when asking for help, demonstrating dictionary use or modelling how to use a story map as a scaffold for rehearsing sentences and as a memory aid for writing.

## 5. Team teaching

To maximise the time spent supporting learning at levels appropriate to your EAL learners' needs, you could consider splitting your class into smaller groups from the outset of a lesson rather than spending any time on whole class work. If you have other adults then each adult can lead a group. This can be really helpful for all learners to be supported with suitably challenging work. If this is not appropriate in your setting then you could consider deploying your support staff in a number of ways during any whole class teaching times:

- observations – checking language use, listening skills and eye contact;
- echoing the teacher – repeating key phrases (in the home language when possible);
- talk partner – leading discussion tasks as a model of Standard English;
- practice partner – chance for EAL learners to practise responses before sharing these to build confidence.

Varying the approaches used with EAL learners during teaching time will help to ensure that they do not become over-reliant on a single supporting strategy.

## 6. Post teaching

Directly after teacher input, ask support staff to recap any key concepts, reminding EAL learners what has been taught. During this time, support staff can ask EAL learners to recap self-help strategies as well as demonstrating language skills by explaining their understanding; and they can intervene by rephrasing learners' responses or reframing key concepts with appropriate visual or physical support if needed. Even older learners can be confused, and perhaps make slower progress if there are different approaches to giving help. Make sure all staff and learners are familiar with the range of self-help independence strategies and are reminded of these as they work through tasks. When group or independent tasks are complete, you might deploy other adults to help check and improve EAL learners' work. Ask support staff to listen to EAL learners read a section of their own writing for instance, or to check vocabulary development by matching words with definitions to support comprehension.

The following lesson activities and the suggested approaches could all be tackled by other adults. Can you suggest any further ideas for deploying support staff effectively?

| | Pre-teaching | Team teaching | Post teaching |
|---|---|---|---|
| **Correcting spellings** | | Clap out individual syllables | Show learners dictionary skills |
| **Labelling maps in geography** | Read and repeat key names | | Ask EAL learners to read labels aloud and find in atlas to self-check |
| **Timeline of historical events** | Using images to illustrate events and match vocabulary to this | | Check understanding by sequencing chronological language |
| **Solving calculations** | Read and repeat mathematical language | Practice partner – explain selected method to solve problem(s) | |

**A spot of theory**

*According to Masci (2008), research into time spent on tasks in schools indicates that success in learning is a combination of instructional time and task time. Effective teachers plan time very carefully and provide clear guidance, routines and instructions to ensure that tasks can be completed and that no learning time is lost or wasted. For EAL learners this can mean more useful time spent learning and applying English language skills.*

# Strategy: Sharing success

In this section the focus is on noticing when these targets are accomplished as well as maximising opportunities to practise and achieve any language goals. To make sure that you assess progress, it is useful to consider all possible steps EAL learners might take in their learning journey. In speaking and listening for instance, this will range from initiating eye contact and use of gestures to speaking confidently. Keeping a detailed record of the small steps will help you share success with the other adults, and there may be success which other adults share with you. It helps you know more helpful information about your learners and most importantly might help EAL learners see their own success in their English language learning journey.

## 7. Sticky situations

No doubt you know just how busy a teacher's day is and how difficult it can be to find opportunities to talk to support staff who might be working between classes and with a number of different learners. Why not further develop the independence of your EAL learners by providing sets of sticky notes on which they can keep a record of their language progress? Older learners can keep their own record and other adults could be deployed to support younger learners. This would be especially effective if you add a challenge like 100 words in 100 days – or even more depending on the skills the EAL learners demonstrate.

## 8. Catch the overlap

As busy teachers it is important that you find effective ways to ensure that EAL learners' progress is shared – through sticky notes and journals, for instance; but it is also vital that any support targeted at helping learners to catch up with their peers is also part of the planned teaching too. If EAL learners are given extra reading support, such as phonics catch-up lessons to develop blending and segmenting skills, teachers should plan opportunities for those learners to demonstrate this in other lessons. Application of skills across and within lessons serves to reinforce and validate the teaching which is happening outside of the usual classroom opportunities. For example, if learners are working on phonics outside of the classroom, you can ensure that any reading or writing tasks developed in your whole class or group teaching include examples of the high frequency words and/or the new phonemes learned.

## 9. Keeping a record

When you are encouraging the development of EAL learners it is vital that speaking, listening, reading and writing are supported effectively, as these four areas are the key to accessing other curriculum subjects. To ensure EAL learners make progress in their language and literacy acquisition, you might create a grid outlining the smaller steps to consider when developing each of these four essential skills. Keeping this running record of progress can help you to target those EAL learners who need additional help to develop their skill in one or more of those areas. For instance, some learners might demonstrate effective listening skills by following instructions but need to develop spoken language skills as they are currently only using single words or phrases they have copied. Highlighting each aspect on a grid can help to quickly identify uneven pictures of progress, and indicate which aspects could be built into teaching and learning to accelerate progress.

The smaller stages which effective speaking and listening might be broken into are included in this partially completed table.

| | Learner A | Learner B | Learner C |
|---|---|---|---|
| **Listening: Shows eye contact** | Observed | | |
| **Speaking and listening: Repeats words and phrases** | | | |
| **Speaking: Uses gestures** | | | Explaining to friends |
| **Listening: Responds to questions** | Daily | Daily – only simple questions | Daily |
| **Spoken language is understandable** | | When talking about familiar routines | |
| **Word order is understandable** | | | |
| **Initiates short conversations** | Every day | | |

You might then use this grid to help set targets for your EAL learners, and you might include dates for your records.

**A spot of theory**

In their influential work on formative assessment which started in 1998, Paul Black and Dylan Wiliam note that improving assessment and therefore attainment for learners is not straightforward and cannot be simplified as a single approach. What they do highlight importantly though is that within their research a central question was raised by effective teachers: do I know enough about my learners? Using different monitoring strategies to gather information about your EAL learners will help you become an effective teacher who can help your individual learners.

**Checklist**

Use this to keep a record of what worked well for you and what didn't. A strategy that works with one learner or group of learners may not work so well with another. Keeping a checklist helps you to work out what factors or learner characteristics call for one approach rather than another. There's a line at the bottom for you to add your own most frequently used strategy, if it's not already included in the list.

| Strategy | Tried it with... | On...(date) | It worked | It didn't work | Worth trying again? |
|---|---|---|---|---|---|
| 1. Setting SMART targets | | | | | |
| 2. Focus on independent learning | | | | | |
| 3. Language expectations: reframing questions and comments | | | | | |
| **4. Pre-teaching\*** | | | | | |
| 5. Team teaching | | | | | |
| 6. Post teaching | | | | | |
| 7. Sticky situations | | | | | |
| 8. Catch the overlap | | | | | |
| 9. Keeping a record | | | | | |
| Your own strategy? | | | | | |

# DAY 6: Progress

## Motivating, monitoring, managing and assessing learning

Assessing the language level and therefore language needs of EAL learners can be complex and time consuming. So for a busy class teacher working with a diverse class, it is essential to be equipped with formative assessment skills which can identify early needs quickly as well as having a skill set to support each group of EAL learners appropriately. The diversity and complexity of these learners' needs may lead to anxiety for even the most experienced of teachers. Recognising that the new-to-English learner may have little or no English is only the first step when new starters begin in a class. Ensuring that these learners are engaged in meaningful and productive learning tasks while simultaneously teaching and developing other learners may feel daunting, especially if the EAL learner seems nervous themselves.

All learners need regular and continued support to remain motivated, and seeing their own progress is one of the central ways this can be achieved. You need to be aware of how the class is getting on and how well the approaches you are using are working to support this. You need to develop decision-making skills to choose when to allow EAL learners to practise independently, and when it might be best to tune in to help monitor and motivate. You can find support within your class by encouraging collaboration and keeping clear records of progress which will motivate them.

The strategies presented today are aimed at supporting you with ways to keep a record of useful evidence of the EAL learners' progress in your classroom. Your school will have its own expectations of record-keeping

approaches but to help you to track and understand your EAL learners' progress in detail, this chapter offers some strategies which can be added to these. The strategies included on Day 6 are designed to:

A. help you think of ways to sustain the motivation of EAL learners who might feel sensitive about their developing language skills;

B. illustrate the importance of baseline assessments;

C. offer ideas for monitoring EAL learners and some additional ways of managing the evidence collected.

### Today's strategies

* Starting out:
  1. I nominate…
  2. Language baseline
  3. Literacy baseline
  4. Cross-curricular baselines

* Collecting and monitoring progress:
  5. Work sampling
  6. Ace assessments
  7. Make it yourself

* Managing the information:
  8. Another brick in the wall(paper)…!
  9. Assess and adjust
  10. Deciphering data

## Strategy: Starting out

EAL learners may develop spoken English language skills for social settings quickly but the journey to their success is more challenging when reading, writing and the wider curriculum are considered. Even small steps can represent progress for EAL learners and monitoring, so managing and assessing this progress is vital to ensure that:

* expectations are being met;
* appropriate support is offered;
* learning improves and that best practice is utilised to move learning forward.

Seeing progress is something that can motivate teachers and learners alike and is developed from having an understanding of learners' prior knowledge. Once you have a clear understanding of the EAL learners' prior knowledge across the curriculum, this can be used to set targets and motivate further success.

### 1. I nominate...

Classroom chatter is normal, and for EAL learners it is very helpful of course, so you can tap into this resource by asking classmates to nominate each other to answer key questions. This is particularly useful when paired or group activities have been used in the lesson and can be a very quick way of finding out the prior knowledge of your EAL learners. Paired learners are well placed to listen to each other and recognise each other's successes. Using peer nomination gives learners the chance to indicate what they have been doing as well as an opportunity to promote esteem.

### 2. Language baseline

A language baseline can include asking questions in English such as the learner's name, about their family and about their home country, especially when you work with new-to-English learners. When you work with more confident EAL learners, you need to be conscious that even when you assess your EAL learners' spoken vocabulary there are other aspects of language which can tell you more about the learners' understanding of English. You need to listen out for pronunciation, language variety, speech structure and fluency. You should check fluency and coherence to ascertain how well ideas are put together in conversations and whether an appropriate spoken speed is used. Language checks can be really useful for older EAL learners who might need to make use of their developing English in a wide range of social and even working contexts.

### 3. Literacy baseline

Before considering how much your EAL learners can read, you must check understanding of the conventions of print in English. Start by checking how your EAL learners hold a book, looking at which way the book is opened. If it is from the left then you need to demonstrate that print in English is read from left to right rather than from right to left as is the case in some languages. Early checks of pencil grips and tracing standard letter forms used in English can also show how experienced the EAL learners are with first language learning, as well as giving the opportunity for some to start to practise letter formation, especially if this is very different from English as is the case with characters used in Mandarin. From here you can use flash cards and simple texts to check reading and dictate passages for writing, having gained a clear understanding of the true baseline.

## 4. Cross-curricular baselines

Assessing knowledge and skills in other subject areas can be fairly straightforward if the subject demands less reading or writing. Even for subjects like history, a baseline can be noted through using picture evidence or sequencing activities. It is vital to note what these are showing so that you can then set appropriate targets and share these with the learners. Calculations in mathematics for instance will of course indicate what EAL learners know about number and number operations, but at the same time will show you the calculation strategies the EAL learner applies. The approaches for solving division may be very different from country to country. It is essential then to think about what you want to assess in a subject: application of the skill or knowledge of a particular strategy?

**A spot of theory**

*Guy Claxton's ongoing work on* Building Learning Power *(2002) indicates the value of helping learners to succeed by recognising what the learners' actual needs are and using this to help develop appropriate targets. Sharing baseline information with your EAL learners can help ensure that their learning power develops.*

**Strategy in action**

Keeping useful evidence to help you check the progress of EAL is especially important when you are tracking the small steps. Year 4 teacher Catherine created her own table for the EAL learners in her class. The following table provides an example of the cross-curricular baseline assessment Catherine uses as a record of the EAL learners' progress. This section considers skills and knowledge in mathematics. Use the expectations within the national curriculum to help create your own.

| Mathematics approach | Baseline observations | Next steps |
| --- | --- | --- |
| *Should be using short division method.* <br><br> *Use formal layout of written multiplication.* | *Ahmed solved division calculations mentally – answer was correct but jottings not included.* <br><br> *To solve the multiplication questions some written work was used but the longer multiplication questions did not show two steps.* | *Keep challenging Ahmed with mental calculations but model making jottings to encourage him to show workings.* <br><br> *Give Ahmed targets of recording each step.* |

# Strategy: Collecting and monitoring progress

The importance of ensuring learners make progress is central to your role as a teacher. You can monitor a range of different facets of learning. This includes knowledge and understanding of key learning; skill development; application of prior knowledge; and learner motivation and effort. For some learners, progress is easily measured through the data gathered in tests or exams. This may be the case for EAL learners who are able to complete assessments alongside their peers, but for some EAL learners you need to think more carefully and creatively about ways to collect and monitor the progress. English language and literacy skills will still be developing and will develop continually. Standardised assessments may not be appropriate for EAL learners, particularly those who are new to English. Thinking of other ways that learners can independently show understanding of key concepts will make a difference in recognising the smaller steps to success that EAL learners are making.

## 5. Work sampling

You may be able to collect evidence of progress which can be shared as a central resource for comparisons. Copies of EAL learners' work in different subjects can be stored easily and used as a reference to help other teachers to understand the progress being made by EAL learners at different stages of English. Keep examples of writing from across the curriculum and include annotations to identify the age, experiences and background information for the EAL learner. The more information you can gather on different groups of learners, the better equipped you are to support individual needs now and in the future.

## 6. Ace assessments

For school-based assessment of learning, it is a good idea to ensure that the assessments reflect the day-to-day experiences of the EAL learners. Unless you are specifically assessing memory, your EAL learners will be better able to demonstrate developing skills and knowledge by using the resources and equipment they usually access to help them complete tasks. It can be really helpful to outline to the EAL learner what you are assessing, and what help they will be given (as well as what they will not). Key to organising effective assessments for EAL learners is to consider:

- what you want the learner to demonstrate;
- how they have been able to practise this so far.

A little extra planning to personalise the assessment will help EAL learners demonstrate their knowledge and understanding.

## 7. Make it yourself

Tests and assessments are challenging for learners, but writing the test is just as tricky. When producing a test there are various considerations needed to ensure the test is appropriate for your EAL learners. First, you need to think about what you want to test or assess and how you want to assess this. Writing is often the dominant mode of assessment in the classroom. However, this might not be the most appropriate mode for your EAL learners, as writing can be subjective and all learners may not be starting from the same level. Making sure that you have developed descriptors and criteria to help you check understanding and indicating what you are expecting will help you to ensure that your assessments are fair and will produce valid and objective evidence which may be used by others where appropriate.

Mary has been developing reading skills with a group of new-to-English EAL learners in her Year 6 English lessons. She focused on fiction for the first half term and explored story structures using story maps, oral retelling and reordering to teach typical story sequences. Mary developed her own test after thinking about what she really wanted the EAL learners to demonstrate. This outline shows her expectations and the way she plans to test her EAL learners:

EAL learners discuss a story sequence.

| Key learning this term? | Focus of assessment? | Independent assessment task? |
|---|---|---|
| Story sequences – beginning, middle and end | Recall of story sequence | Reordering a known story (some will need key pictures from the text to help) |

### A spot of theory

*In 1990 Hilary Hester identified four different developmental stages for EAL learners' competence in English, with Stage 4 incorporating the aim of fluent use of English in a range of social and learning contexts. The first two stages include new-to-English and becoming familiar with language and in Stage 3 a learner might demonstrate success in subjects like mathematics and science but may continue to need additional language support.*

## Strategy: Managing the information

Data collection is only part of the process needed to monitor and assess EAL learners' attainment and progress. Using this data to identify any gaps – which may be learning or language linked – and to direct future progress is even more important. Identifying special educational needs can be difficult when working with EAL learners because these might be confused with language needs. A key to understanding and interpreting the data for your EAL learners is recognising that your EAL learners might be from different home countries, meaning that their education experiences are likely to be different. Use your data wisely to identify any gaps and strengths for individuals. Some EAL learners may be demonstrating success in some of the curriculum subjects, making it your goal to understand why and how this success can be translated to other areas.

## 8. Another brick in the wall(paper)...!

A large display in the form of a 'brick wall' can be useful as a learning wall to keep achievements visible for EAL learners. Each brick can represent a key learning objective, which can be added to gradually to create a 'wall of success' showing learners the progress they are making in the English language journey they are undertaking. You might use the bricks as a record of a target if you challenge EAL learners to learn a numbered amount of new vocabulary in a set number of days.

## 9. Assess and adjust

Using assessment for learning strategies is a part of your daily teaching. When you work with EAL learners, you might be concerned with ensuring language is developed continually and feel pressure to ensure that new language is introduced at all points. Language development and progress is crucial but remember that practice really can make perfect. If your EAL learners struggle with new concepts in your lessons then take a little time to adjust your lesson and recap on the language which has already been developed. Even spending ten minutes reminding EAL learners of language they have previously learned can be useful in helping learners move forward.

## 10. Deciphering data

Making effective use of data obviously starts with scrutinising which EAL learners are meeting the expectations and which are not; but from there much more detailed unpicking needs to be used to work out how to move each EAL learner forward. Vital to this is remembering that your EAL learners are influenced by a range of factors outside of the learning environment. You might need to create your own spreadsheet to ensure all influences are considered, including:

- date of entry to UK;
- first language;
- academic knowledge/application of first language;
- work rate.

Appropriate targets can be set for individual EAL learners when relevant background information is available to support these.

In a primary school the data on EAL learners is scrutinised every half term and mapped out to indicate where best to place any additional support for the following half term.

For example in Year 1 it looks like this:

| Year group / numbers of EAL learners | New starters making progress? | Use of mother tongue? | Other curriculum areas? | Work rate? | Targets? |
|---|---|---|---|---|---|
| Year 1:<br><br>9 EAL learners<br><br>2 Polish, 3 Czech, 4 Urdu. | *Yes – 2 new starters, both Polish.* | Polish and Czech use this spoken only – parents advise that children have access to books; Urdu learners read Arabic too and read English. | × 1 Czech learner and × 1 Polish learner finding maths and science difficult, as well as not following instructions in PE. | All learners show positive attitudes to learning. | Focus on reading – holding books and reading left to right – all EAL; dual language books – Polish and Czech. |

Unpicking data for individual EAL learners and different language groups can help to personalise learning and target support where it is really needed.

**A spot of theory**

*Mistry and Sood (2012) identified the importance of careful collection of data for monitoring and tracking the progress of EAL learners: 'It is only through having [such] robust data captured and analysed throughout the school year that confidence in [pupil] attainment can be made' (Mistry and Sood, 2012, p 285). Collection of all data – even the smallest steps – helps to provide a clear and detailed picture of EAL learners' progress.*

**If you only try one thing from this chapter, try this\***

**Checklist**

Use this to keep a record of what worked well for you and what didn't. A strategy that works with one learner or group of learners may not work so well with another. Keeping a checklist helps you to work out what factors or learner characteristics call for one approach rather than another. There's a line at the bottom for you to add your own most frequently used strategy, if it's not already included in the list.

| Strategy | Tried it with... | On...(date) | It worked | It didn't work | Worth trying again? |
|---|---|---|---|---|---|
| 1. I nominate... | | | | | |
| 2. Language baseline | | | | | |
| 3. Literacy baseline | | | | | |
| 4. Cross-curricular baselines | | | | | |
| 5. Work sampling | | | | | |
| 6. Ace assessments | | | | | |
| 7. Make it yourself | | | | | |
| 8. Another brick in the wall(paper)...! | | | | | |
| 9. Assess and adjust | | | | | |
| **10. Deciphering data\*** | | | | | |
| Your own strategy? | | | | | |

50

# DAY 7: Beyond language support

## Understanding cultural differences and emotional needs

EAL learners may have similar needs to those whose first language is English, ranging from special educational needs to supporting giftedness and everything in between. However, you need to remember that this group of learners have some distinctive needs resulting from differing cultural backgrounds as well as recognise that the journey for English language acquisition is a lengthy process which is rewarding but requires motivation in the learners. The expectations and understanding that different cultures and communities have of education, developing language skills and approaches to learning impact on individual learners and may sharply contrast with your own experiences. There may be contrasts in motivation, home and family support, alongside beliefs in the value of school.

As a teacher you should consider that migrant worker families are likely to experience social and economic upheaval when relocating; and that there are families of asylum seekers and refugees who may have experienced emotional and mental distress. This final chapter provides straightforward suggestions for understanding and celebrating these differences and some ideas to help you begin to meet the emotional needs resulting from a range of experiences. Sensitivity to difference helps to broaden perspectives and understand different cultures, languages and countries. Learners could have a range of feelings about their other language or languages, ranging from positive, excited, negative, confident or sensitive. As a teacher of EAL learners, you may find that sharing the differences can help to improve awareness and most importantly help all learners appreciate and understand the experiences of people from other cultures.

The strategies presented here could be used to develop mutual understanding which benefits learners and teachers alike.

- Be culture vultures:
  1. Save the date
  2. Language for days
  3. What did you say?
  4. Food glorious food

- Look, listen and learn:
  5. Window on the world
  6. The Skype's the limit
  7. Show 'em how it's done!
  8. Fantastic film club

- Let's get together:
  9. Talk Tuesdays
  10. Extending befriending
  11. Delve into drama
  12. Sporting greats

## Strategy: Be culture vultures

Gathering information about a learner can obviously help you to understand individual needs, and if this is combined with knowledge of a country and culture then you can more confidently understand your EAL learners' experiences and backgrounds. Asking your EAL learners about their home countries might be difficult at first, but by finding out a little more about different countries you can effectively develop common ground for talk. There are common themes such as national holidays like Christmas and special festivals in different countries, and common language such as the days of the week. Sharing celebrations and celebratory foods can be very useful in developing your school community. Talk in your school can include first language talk, especially if your school plans to celebrate the annual International Mother Tongue day – on 21 February each year.

### 1. Save the date

A school calendar can remind all learners of key dates such as term dates and holidays. Adding significant dates remembered or celebrated in different countries around the world is a simple but effective inclusion strategy. Known dates – such as national holidays – might be added when the calendar is produced but this could also be a class activity at the start of a year or when new EAL learners are welcomed into the class. The school website could also include the calendar to raise awareness and illustrate that the learning environment welcomes and celebrates diversity. A calendar of key dates is useful for teachers too as it helps to plan for integrating celebrations into the day or when learners might be absent because they are celebrating significant festivals or for religious observance.

### 2. Language for days

To make your cultural calendar even more inclusive you could include the names of days and months in different languages. The days of the week and months of the year have different names all over the world, so including those from the languages represented in your school is really helpful to ensure EAL learners not only are included but also have a clear knowledge of important term dates. You might use a different language for each week or month, or to challenge older learners task them with finding out different translations to help in the production of a calendar.

### 3. What did you say?

A 'Language of the Month' display could be positioned in a central area of your classroom or school to welcome learners and families and show that diversity is valued. The display could include: maps to illustrate where the chosen language is spoken; images of any significant buildings or landmarks; and some words and phrases (such as hello, goodbye and thank you) in the chosen language. Leaflets could be provided for interested learners to find out more about the language and where it is spoken. Over time you should try to ensure that all languages represented in your school or classroom are included. This could be further developed by asking the EAL learners to record examples of the correct pronunciation of the key words and phrases, or even to help with the teaching of these.

### 4. Food glorious food

Celebrations are often accompanied by food. You could hold a food festival with your EAL learners to help welcome different cultures into your school. Food festivals can be held as often as you might like, possibly tied in with the Language of the Month or specific events celebrated by your EAL learners from different countries. You could ask EAL learners to bring in foods traditionally eaten during festive occasions like Christmas or birthdays. You might ask EAL learners to contribute foods or even ask older EAL learners to demonstrate making the foods if you provide the ingredients for them. This is a useful opportunity for all learners to broaden their international perspectives.

## Strategy in action

Katie created a Language of the Month board as a corridor display. She has EAL learners from five different European countries in her Year 4 class. She decided to use the same set of key words and phrases for every language and listed these in English alongside the new language as a further opportunity to reinforce English for the EAL learners in her class.

| Days of the week | Hello, Goodbye, How are you? | Food names |
|---|---|---|
| Months of the year | Please and Thank you | Jobs |

Katie's EAL learners appreciated this language display and helped her to develop it further by explaining which words or phrases they wanted more support with. What might this look like in your classroom?

### A spot of theory

Blanca Araujo's 2009 article 'Best Practices in Working with Linguistically Diverse Families' highlights the benefits of culturally relevant teaching. She explains that extending English learning opportunities into the wider school community and accepting help from this community can lead to better communication and academic success in EAL learners.

## Strategy: Look, listen and learn

Information about education systems around the world is widely available thanks to the internet, and of course you can find out more from the EAL learners and their families. You can extend the multicultural view of your classroom by making use of technology, which is at yours and your learners' fingertips nowadays. You can look online at available school websites or at images from the tourist websites from other countries. Establishing a global classroom partner is really beneficial to help you see how teaching and learning happens around the world, which of course supports your learners to develop a multicultural perspective.

## 5. Window on the world

The view from your own classroom window might be very familiar, but every classroom is different. You can enhance the understanding of other countries further by making use of technology to help explore real views that learners might see from their classroom windows in different countries. A simple art or photography project to embrace different cultures involves asking your learners to create a picture, either from memory or using photographs of the view from their first classroom window. The differences between classroom views around the world might be explored and the idea links well with subjects like geography and creative arts. This is a very useful first project to undertake with a global partner.

## 6. The Skype's the limit

Developing global partnerships can be facilitated through different channels, but one which would be hugely beneficial would be with a school known by some of the learners or their families. Learners and families might have contacts to help with this, and with facilities like Skype or FaceTime, global partnerships today offer first-hand virtual views of life in other countries. To make the most of global links you can compare an experience – which is much easier if you are able to see it. This might start on a small scale through comparing how the linked institutions have decorated for Christmas or another celebration. Beyond this you could share stories, ask questions and even team teach lessons with the global partner school or college.

## 7. Show 'em how it's done

The EAL learners in your school or college will have expectations of education influenced by their own experiences or those of their families. For some the approaches used in the UK system, such as group work or discussion-based tasks, are very different from the teaching styles used in their home country. You can explore this with a global partner through setting shared challenges ranging from maths problems to performing Shakespeare, depending on the age of your learners. With a global partner you might set each other challenges and share regular updates on how these are being approached, helping to extend global awareness.

## 8. Fantastic film club

Films are popular worldwide and EAL learners are likely to have seen several English language films. Schools and colleges often have extra-curricular clubs for learners and a film club can be a very popular one. The idea would be to share the film and hosting a discussion afterwards. Foreign language films with subtitles are widely available online so you could include films from different countries as a regular feature in the film club. The choice is endless really but you could start with short animated films from different countries, which often have universal appeal unrestricted by age – especially if it reminds an older learner of growing up in their home country!

Sally teaches Year 2 in an inner city school. The school has a large number of children from economic migrant families. The economic migrant families are a growing community but sometimes EAL learners can feel a bit isolated or even homesick. Sally is in her second year of teaching after having a successful NQT year. During her first year she started an after school film club. Initially this was to share her own love of films but as the club grew she started to ask the club members for recommendations and realised she could broaden learners' perspectives by including films from around the world. Sally started by searching for popular children's cartoons from around the world and in particular from some of the countries familiar to the EAL learners. She shared the animated films to the delight of the club. The EAL learners contributed by making recommendations and more confident and advanced English speakers even presented some background information about the cartoons or films, starting discussions about their favourites. This has become one of Sally's favourite parts of the week, and helps the EAL learners in the club feel valued as part of the school community.

### A spot of theory

*In Feyisa Demie's short paper from 2001: 'Ethnic and Gender Differences in Educational Attainment', she states: 'Ethnic heritage does not presuppose underachievement' (Demie, 2001, p 2). Background information on education systems in different countries experienced first hand through partnerships can support understanding of this important statement and avoid incorrect assumptions about learner potential.*

*EAL learners discuss their favourite foreign language cartoons.*

## Strategy: Let's get together

Strategies to extend opportunities for English language development will of course be helped by effective home/school relationships, but sometimes this can be difficult because of a range of challenging variables. A school can make a difference beyond the classroom and is sometimes best placed to do this as a central hub where a community can come together to share cultural experiences and interests. Community events can be regular or one-off, large or small scale. As a note of caution it is important to be sensitive about the issues which EAL learners and their families might be facing. These can range from economic uncertainty to seeking refugee status. As a class teacher you will be in the best position to decide which topics can and should be explored. The following strategies could help get you started in exploring issues and creating a cohesive community within your class or year group.

## 9. Talk Tuesdays

Regular coffee mornings for your school or class can help to develop a cultural community. Talk Tuesdays (or any day of the week!) can easily be organised within your class and are an opportunity to share key information with families, to signpost the community towards others who can provide essential guidance on available support for EAL learners or their families, and to better understand the needs of the different groups in a community. As a class teacher you can organise small events to help showcase the learners' work and help families understand how EAL learners are developing their English skills alongside other curriculum areas. When a regular community event becomes established, the community themselves may begin to take the lead.

## 10. Extending befriending

Learning English is essential to communicate socially, to construct relationships and to understand the systems and procedures of a community, including a school or college community. A buddy can help individual EAL learners to achieve these skills and this can be extended to families to help members of the wider community with any support they might need. This is especially helpful for families of new starters within your class. Ask the wider community if anybody can volunteer to help support the families of new starters. This might be managed through a volunteer board in the entrance area of the classroom or school building, or perhaps on the school website or social media where contact details of volunteers could be shared.

## 11. Delve into drama

Using dramatic techniques in the classroom can be very useful to help understand characters. There are a wide range of popular dramatic techniques you can use to help explore emotions and motivations, for example through asking questions using hotseating, but forum theatre could be especially helpful if you are considering the complicated issues faced by some of the EAL learners in your classroom. In forum theatre the scene is acted out twice. During the second showing the scene can be stopped by any of the audience – or your class. The idea is that they offer alternative suggestions for the outcome of the scene. This would be a very effective way of encouraging other learners to recognise some of the sensitive issues which EAL learners could face.

## 12. Sporting greats

Extra-curricular sports clubs are common in schools and colleges and are sometimes extended to the wider community. If you run a sports club you might advertise it in a different language to facilitate universal appeal, but you can further interest EAL learners through sharing famous figures from the sport from around the world. Sports like football are popular around the world and players in famous clubs like Manchester United could come from a range of different countries. Different countries might have favourite sports – you can use this to find out what sports club might be popular with your EAL learners, or even as a starting point for discussion or writing activities.

**A spot of theory**

*When Laura Day Ashley explored the use of forum theatre workshops to help students understand issues faced by refugees, she reflected that the drama helped the learners to consider the feelings of others and to recognise the difficulties which refugees might face. She recommends follow-up discussion activities to avoid a feeling of one-off drama workshops and offer learners the chance to use the skills they develop in these sorts of reflective dramas.*

**Strategy in action**

Matthew displays a wall chart in his Year 5 classroom of the different sports followed by all of the learners in his class. At the start of the year he used visual prompts and a simple thumbs-up/thumbs-down response to find out what his class liked. The wall chart is interactive and all learners are encouraged to note any successes their favourite teams or individuals have had. Matthew finds that after a weekend his class will come in and add to the wall chart. He has noticed that the EAL learners talk more confidently in his class because of a shared interest, and that all learners are interested to find out where their favourite players and teams originate.

Matthew's wallchart looks like this:

|  | Football | Cricket | Tennis | Basketball |
|---|---|---|---|---|
| **Popular in which countries?** |  |  |  |  |
| **Favourite teams and players?** |  |  |  |  |
| **Who is winning?** |  |  |  |  |

This is easily adapted to tap into the interests of your class or form group. Which sports would be on yours?

Use this to keep a record of what worked well for you and what didn't. A strategy that works with one learner or group of learners may not work so well with another. Keeping a checklist helps you to work out what factors or learner characteristics call for one approach rather than another. There's a line at the bottom for you to add your own most frequently used strategy, if it's not already included.

| Strategy | Tried it with … | On…(date) | It worked | It didn't work | Worth trying again? |
|---|---|---|---|---|---|
| **1. Save the date\*** | | | | | |
| 2. Language for days | | | | | |
| 3. What did you say? | | | | | |
| 4. Food glorious food | | | | | |
| 5. Window on the world | | | | | |
| 6. The Skype's the limit | | | | | |
| 7. Show 'em how it's done | | | | | |
| 8. Fantastic film club | | | | | |
| 9. Talk Tuesdays | | | | | |
| 10. Extending befriending | | | | | |
| 11. Delve into drama | | | | | |
| 12. Sporting greats | | | | | |
| Your own strategy? | | | | | |

# Further reading

## General education literature

Bandura, A (1977) Self-Efficacy: Toward a Unifying Theory of Behavioural Change. *Psychological Review,* 84: 191–215.

Baumfield, V and Mroz, M (2002) Investigating Pupils' Questions in the Primary Classroom. *Educational Research,* 44(2): 129–40.

Black, P and Wiliam, D (1998) Inside the Black Box: Raising Standards Through Classroom Assessment. *Phi Delta Kappan,* 80(2): 139–48.

Bruner, J (1996) *The Culture of Education.* London: Harvard University Press.

Claxton, G (2002) *Building Learning Power: Helping Young People Become Better Learners.* Bristol, England: TLO Limited

Hattie, J (2008) *Visible Learning: A Synthesis of Over 800 Meta-Analyses Relating to Achievement.* Oxon, England: Routledge.

Masci, F (2008) Time for Time on Task and Quality Instruction. *Middle School Journal,* 40(2): 33–41.

Mercer, N, Warwick, P and Ahmed, A (2013–14) *The Cambridge Oracy Project.* [online] Available at: https://thinkingtogether. educ.cam.ac.uk/downloads/oracy2014/The_Cambridge_Oracy_ Assessment_Project.pdf (accessed 10 April 2018).

Pica, R (1999) *Moving & Learning across the Curriculum.* Albany, NY: Delmar Publishers.

Vygotsky, L (1986) *Thought and Language* (edited by Alex Kozulin). London: MIT Press.

## EAL-focused theory and research

Araujo, B (2009) Best Practices in Working with Linguistically Diverse Families. *Intervention in School and Clinic*, 45(2): 116–23. [online] Available at: http://journals.sagepub.com/doi/pdf/10.1177/ 1053451209340221 (accessed 10 April 2018).

Cummins, J (2000) *Language, Power and Pedagogy: Bilingual Children in the Crossfire* (Bilingual Education & Bilingualism). Clevedon, England: Multilingual Matters.

Day Ashley, L (2002) 'Putting Yourself in Other People's Shoes': the use of Forum theatre to explore refugee and homeless issues in schools,' *Journal of Moral Education*, 31, 1, 21–34. ISSN: 0305-7240: http://dx.doi. org/10.1080/03057240120111418"DOI: 10.1080/03057240120111418

Demie, F (2013) English as an Additional Language Pupils: How Long Does It Take to Acquire English Fluency? *Language and Education*, 27(1): 59–69.

Dickinson, D K and Tabors, P O (2001) *Beginning Literacy with Language: Young Children Learning at Home and School.* Baltimore, MD: Brookes Publishing.

Gibbons, P (1993) *Learning to Learn in a Second Language.* Portsmouth, NH: Heinemann.

Gibbons, P (2002) *Scaffolding Language, Scaffolding Learning: Teaching Second Language Learners in the Mainstream Classroom.* Portsmouth, NH: Heinemann.

Hester, H (1990) *Patterns of Learning*. London: CLPE.

Letters and Sounds: Principles and Practice of High Quality Phonics. Primary National Strategy: Crown Copyright (2007) [online] https://assets.publishing.service.gov.uk/government/uploads/system/uploads/attachment_data/file/190599/Letters_and_Sounds_-_DFES-00281-2007.pdf (last accessed 18/4/18).

Mistry, M and Sood, K (2012) Raising Standards for Pupils Who Have English as an Additional Language (EAL) through Monitoring and Evaluation of Provision in Primary Schools. *Education 3–13: International Journal of Primary, Elementary and Early Years Education*, 40(3): 281–93.

Misty Adoniou, M (2013) Drawing to Support Writing Development in English Language Learners. *Language and Education*, 27(3): 261–77.

NALDIC (2016) EAL Learners in the UK: Who are Our EAL Learners? [online], https://naldic.org.uk/the-eal-learner/eal-learners-uk (accessed 18 April 2018).

NALDIC (1999) The Distinctiveness of English as an Additional Language: A Cross-Curriculum Discipline. *Working Paper 5*. Edited by Hugh South. [online] Available at: www.NALDIC.org (accessed 10 April 2018).

QCA (2000) *A Language in Common: Assessing English as an Additional Language*. [online] Available at: http://dera.ioe.ac.uk/4440/1/3359_language_in_common.pdf (accessed 10 April 2018).

Wardman, C (2013) Interactions between EAL pupils, specialist teachers and TAs during withdrawal from the mainstream in UK primary schools, Education 3–13, 41:6, 647–63.